The Ghost Tour of Great Britain
of Great Britain

Lincolnshire

The Ghost Tour of Great Britain

Lincolnshire

with *Most Haunted's* **Richard Felix**

breedon **books**
PUBLISHING

ACKNOWLEDGEMENTS

The production of this book would not have been possible
without the help and expertise of:

the other members of the Ghost Tour team,

Steve Lilley and Delicia Redfern

Nathan Fearn

and all the staff at Breedon Books in Derby

All photographs Steve Lilley and Delicia Redfern

First published in Great Britain in 2006 by The Breedon Books Publishing Company Limited,
Breedon House, 3 The Parker Centre, Derby, DE21 4SZ.

© Steve Lilley and Richard Felix, 2006
Reprinted 2009

ISBN 978-1-85983-740-5   Printed and bound by TJ International, Padstow, Cornwall.

CONTENTS

NEW YORK 3147

JOHN O'GROATS 874

ISLES OF SCILLY 28
LONGSHIPS LIGHTHOUSE 1½

NATIONAL GHOST
TOUR

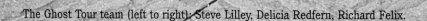

The Ghost Tour team (left to right): Steve Lilley, Delicia Redfern, Richard Felix.

PREFACE

When local historian Richard Felix opened a Heritage Centre in his home city of Derby, England, in 1992, even his far-reaching powers of perception could not have forecast how important a step he had taken.

The Heritage Centre, based in an area of the city known as St Peter's churchyard, became the starting point for Richard's innovative ghost walks and within 12 years more than 150,000 people – many of them so fascinated by the concept that they visited from America – had booked in to be scared out of their wits.

Soon the Derby ghost walks took on legendary status and were attended by scores of would-be ghost hunters. The story unfolds as ghost walkers leave the Heritage Centre and are told that they are walking over the bodies of many of the victims of the Black Death. They head down St Peter's Street towards the site of Derby's first gaol, a place of incarceration for witches, heretics and traitors. The Lock-Up Yard, the scene of the brutal murder of a policeman, is visited next. A moment's reprieve permits the ghost-hunters to partake of another kind of spirit in the Tiger Bar, in preparation for a subterranean trip down into the barrel-vaulted tunnels beneath Derby's Guildhall. The story continues as the party heads across the Market Place, then on to the Cathedral, the Shire Hall (the scene of a horrendous pressing to death in 1665), before returning to the Heritage Centre for a Ghost Hunter's Supper – for those who can stomach the feast that is!

With the success of his ghost tours in Derby it became clear to Richard Felix that a formula that worked so well in one place would probably succeed in other towns and cities across the

British Isles, and so when he was approached by film producer Stephen Lilley to record a remarkable DVD series – *The Ghost Tour of Great Britain* – he jumped at the chance. It was a mammoth, time-consuming task that relied on the great British public taking the idea seriously. And they did. The intrepid pair visited every major city and well over 40 counties throughout England, Scotland, Ireland and Wales and, with incredible attention to detail, they attempted to uncover explanations for each eerie haunting, researching library archives and interviewing credible witnesses, historians, renowned psychics and parapsychologists.

As interest in the ghost walks and *The Ghost Tour of Great Britain* increased, so did Richard Felix's fame as an authority on all things paranormal. He was invited to become the resident historical expert on the hugely popular Living TV show *Most Haunted*. Appropriately, one of the places investigated by *Most Haunted* was Derby Gaol – undoubtedly one of the most haunted sites in Britain. Situated in the basement of 50/51 Friar Gate, Derby Gaol is a working museum where visitors can see the actual cells where prisoners were kept. It was used as a prison from 1756 to 1828 and, following its acquisition by Richard Felix in 1997, has been restored to its original condition. Now visitors can try paranormal investigations using the latest hi-tech ghost-hunting equipment, just as the *Most Haunted* team did on film inside the Condemned Cell. Those of a fearless disposition can even sign up for a Derby Gaol Sleepover, comprising a mini ghost walk for an hour and a half around Friar Gate, a pie and porter supper and a bar that serves all night! A medium can also be arranged to carry out séances and private readings.

This book has been written to accompany the DVD series and recounts in words and pictures the chilling accounts of paranormal experiences uncovered by Richard Felix and Steve Lilley on their groundbreaking trip, *The Ghost Tour of Great Britain*.

PART ONE

GHOSTS
AND HOW
TO FIND
THEM

RICHARD'S THEORIES ABOUT GHOSTS

As I was raised in a haunted house, you will forgive me for having well-formed ideas about the existence of ghosts. After years of study and countless fascinating experiences, some of them truly frightening, I now consider myself an expert in the paranormal.

It may surprise you to learn, therefore, that as a child the very thought of spirits, ghouls and skeletons filled me with fear and dread. I was petrified by ghosts and, to a certain extent, I still am to this day. When I was no more than four years old I was locked into garages and garden sheds by so-called friends and told that the 'Green Ghost' was going to get me. Experiences such as this only served to fuel an already fertile imagination and as a child I would refuse to stay in any building on my own and would certainly never walk past a churchyard alone or even walk upstairs without someone's hand to hold. I spent many a night as a youngster lying wide awake beneath my bedclothes, waiting for a demonic being to stride into my bedroom, pull back the bedclothes and reveal its hideous face. Of course this never happened, but perhaps my way of facing up to my fears was to attempt to discover all I possibly could about how and why spirits haunt places.

In the early 1990s I started to conduct ghost walks around Derby – and 12 years later well over 150,000 people had been on a ghost tour of my home city. Derby's location, almost in the centre of the country, has underlined its great importance for almost 2,000 years and contributed to its prosperity. It has always been a crossing of the ways and was the scene of the last hanging, drawing and quartering to be carried out in England, the result of the last rebellion against the Crown to take place in this country.

However, every region of these isles has its own folklore and legends and in recognition of this Stephen Lilley and I embarked on *The Ghost Tour of Great Britain*. In less than three years we visited nearly every county in the land, looking for ghosts, talking to people who have seen ghosts and visiting haunted places. My experiences as an expert on the popular *Most Haunted* TV programme have broadened my horizons still further and put me in direct contact with the scariest places in Great Britain and beyond. Even today, however, I am still learning and remain grateful to the

folklorists and parapsychologists who continually surprise me with their thoughts and theories.

In this book, you will read chilling tales of hauntings, but I will also attempt to pass on, from my own experiences, the knowledge and details of the equipment you need to detect paranormal activity yourself. In short, everything you need to know to become a ghost-hunter.

First, however, you need to understand what a ghost is.

Some parapsychologists don't believe in life after death and put hauntings down to the influence of the living, not the dead. They attribute unexplained events to Extra Sensory Perception (ESP) – the psychic powers of living individuals who have the ability, for example, to move objects.

We are taught from an early age that we *can't* do certain things. If a door opens by itself, a spoon bends without any force being applied to it or a glass on a mantelpiece suddenly shatters, as adults we look for a logical explanation. Those who believe in ESP say that this desire to explain away inexplicable events is no more than a safety valve – far better to be a sceptic than attribute strange happenings to the power of the mind and run the risk of being ridiculed. And at least ESP and the idea of telepathic understanding between living creatures is a more comfortable theory to swallow than the spectre of the dead being trapped on earth as punishment for terrible crimes or through the tragedy and pain of an unexpected demise.

The idea of sharing our world – sometimes our own homes – with the spirits of dead people is uncomfortable to say the least, but I have met hundreds of sane, sober individuals who swear they have encountered a ghost. Intrigued? Well, before you read on, please make a note of the Richard Felix Rules of Ghost Hunting. First, you have to be an enthusiast. Second, you need to be a detective, and third, most certainly a sceptic. You have to explore all avenues when you look into a ghost's history and get to the bottom of the *reason* for the haunting.

For many, that would be enough. However, I passionately believe the ultimate aim of the ghost-hunter is to ask: 'How can I help?' If you're looking for nothing more than the cheap thrill of a scary experience, go and watch a horror movie. I feel that there's a responsibility attached to ghost-hunting. If an animal lover tracks down a caged gorilla, does he simply take a photograph of the sad ape and walk away? No, that's not enough – the final act has to be to release the creature from its pain. It is therefore important to understand that ghosts – whether the product of the living or the dead – haunt places for different reasons and I believe that there are at least five distinct types.

The dead returning

This is where a spirit is seeking some kind of 'closure', as our American friends might say. It can interact, is aware of its environment and knows you are there – it's a conscious entity that can even speak to you. To me, this is the most frightening type of ghost, but what's the reason for its existence? The basic premise is that while the spirit of a dead person remains on earth, the soul moves on to its eternal reward. So maybe our interactive ghosts have business on earth they haven't concluded or are somehow trapped and can't move on to where good souls go.

In the Middle Ages there was a strong belief in Purgatory – a state in between heaven and hell. Quite often human bones are found where ghosts have been seen for a number of years and a common theory is that troubled souls haunt the earth because they weren't buried properly. The way we depart this life isn't something most of us think too deeply about these days, but in bygone times people craved a decent burial. Could denial of the Last Rites or bitterness that their bones were interred in ground that was not consecrated create the energy of a troubled ghost, stubbornly waiting for a proper burial?

I spoke recently to a Cornish woman who told me that through the Church's influence in the Middle Ages and its warnings of eternal damnation, souls that had done bad deeds in life were simply too afraid to move on, so instead hovered on earth as ghosts.

This theory may help to explain why we don't see many modern ghosts – there was more fear in the past of the punishment for sins in death, hence the reluctance of some to take the step into the afterlife. Perhaps these days we are more relaxed about our wrong-doings and don't believe they have to be paid for when we die?

Some ghosts apparently don't have any choice about whether or not they move on to another place. We have long been told that individuals who have committed terrible crimes are condemned to walk this earth for eternity, repenting their sins. Marley's ghost in Charles Dickens's *A Christmas Carol* warns Scrooge to mend his ways, or face the prospect of dragging in death the heavy chains he has forged link by link throughout his corrupt life.

The fact that these interactive ghosts represent the dead returning and the spirits of real people – entities with intelligence – makes them difficult to track down. Why would a self-respecting ghost with the ability to interact allow itself to be nailed by a gang of hi-tech ghost-hunters wielding laser temperature readers?

The apparition

If you could take a camcorder and video player back in time 200 years, imagine how staggered the people of early 19th-century Britain would be at your ability to play back on a screen a particular event you had just recorded.

So why are we shocked today by the idea of a traumatic event, perhaps a terrible premature death, somehow recording itself naturally into rock, brickwork, or even soil? Stone in particular is an ideal recording medium because it contains silica, and it's my belief that the energy emanates out of the stone.

I believe electronic impulses emanate from the brain in the moments before death takes place, creating energy that imprints itself into the fabric of the location. When atmospheric conditions are right, the image created by this energy replays the scene. That's why you see an apparition as it was just before the person died, but it's no more real than watching John Wayne in an old cowboy movie. The Duke long ago rode off into the sunset to that big ranch in the sky – it's his image you see and hear on video and it's impossible for him to interact with you. The same can be said for apparitions.

The tragic scene is played out again and again, but this ghost can't interact – there's no sense of the apparition being aware of the living. Just like a favourite videotape that is played too often, apparitions tend to fade through time. There are stories of ghostly hauntings that have become less distinct down the years, starting out, for example, as a red lady in the 18th century, changing to a pink lady in the 19th century, then to a white lady in the 20th century before becoming no more than a pillar of light accompanied by the sound of footsteps.

Telepathic projection

Like the apparition, this ghost is created by a moment of crisis. We've all heard stories of the woman who sees the image of her husband stranded on a mountain or a soldier appearing to his family moments before he is killed in the trenches.

These are classic examples of the telepathic understanding between people who love each other. In some cases the person who appears as a 'ghost' doesn't actually die, because their appearance prompts a loved-one to summon help. We have all experienced that nagging voice in our head that tells us to visit a relative or friend we know is sick. It's a telepathic experience linked to high emotion.

Phantasm

This is a bizarre apparition that, some would say, proves that ghosts are as much to do with the living as the dead. In the 1888 Census of Hallucinations, a huge survey, the Society for Psychical Research interviewed people throughout the British Isles and Northern France and came up with a surprising statistic. It was discovered that where those questioned were actually able to identify the ghost they had seen, half of the 'ghosts' were still alive and in no danger at the time they were seen! Phantasms are created by another form of telepathy, where an individual, though alive, somehow places an image of himself elsewhere. Far-fetched? Well I have a first-hand account of a baker who, after he had retired, was seen by the new owner of the business as an apparition going about his duties in the bakery. The new owner assumed that he had seen a ghost and that the old baker must be dead. However, on further investigation he discovered that the old man was very much alive, but had little to do in retirement. Consequently he spent most of his time in solitude, daydreaming about his old job. In doing this he somehow provoked the ghostly image of himself to appear at his beloved bakery to be witnessed by the new owner.

Poltergeist

Poltergeists represent a big group of ghosts. There are two contrasting schools of thought on exactly what makes a poltergeist. The name comes from the mediaeval German words *polte* (noisy) and *geist* (ghost). Once again the definition of this ghost comes down to a battle between the living and the dead. One side of the argument believes poltergeists are mischievous, sometimes malevolent, spirits who inhabit a particular place, often a room. The other side goes with the theory of Recurrent Spontaneous Psycho Kinesis, or RSPK for short. They believe that living people, for reasons we don't understand, use the power of their own minds to affect their environments.

Scary movies have given many people a very definite idea of what poltergeists do. We have been drip-fed an image of mischievous spirits throwing objects across rooms, but poltergeist hauntings tend to be more measured than the cinematic interpretation suggests. More regularly they start with a scratching sound and then move on to the odd loud bang, progressing to unpleasant smells. Eventually objects start to move – not initially by floating across a room, but in an annoying way. A set of house keys you always leave on the kitchen table disappears, you hunt high and low and half an hour later you find them – exactly where you left them.

Then come phenomena known as 'small object displacement'. Everyday objects disappear from a room and reappear in a different place. The next stage of a poltergeist haunting is that unusual items appear from nowhere. Old wooden toys, teddy bears, and, at its most grisly, human bones, have all been reported as appearing in rooms. Eventually poltergeist activity progresses to the classic image of objects flying across a room. It's interesting to note though that objects in these reported cases are said to float in straight lines, rather than going up and down in an arc the way they would if you or I threw something in the air and let gravity take charge.

I have very seldom spoken to anyone who has been damaged physically or mentally by ghosts – nor have I heard of poltergeist activity resulting in objects actually hitting anyone. I believe poltergeist activity isn't either mischievous or malevolent, but a call for help. The longest poltergeist incidence I have encountered is a year, but more usually it's a matter of weeks or months.

Filming one episode of *Most Haunted*, our camera captured a teddy bear flying across a room where a child had died many years before.

It seems that poltergeists focus either on a particular person or on a particular place. I have spoken to parapsychologists who have totally sealed off a room where poltergeist activity had been reported. They left a camera running and there was absolutely no possible way the room could be interfered with by any living being. They waited outside and within a minute heard a huge smashing sound. Running into the room, they found the camera pointing at the floor and a teddy bear, last seen on a sofa, sitting with its paws up in front of the fire, as if to warm itself against the cold.

Quite often, poltergeist cases seem to have a living agent. It's normally people who are highly intelligent, creative and imaginative, possibly disturbed by family issues. It is claimed that emotionally charged individuals troubled, for example, by the onset of puberty, cause some poltergeist experiences. That is why it is so important to map out family relationships and areas where an individual might be emotionally charged before diving in with theories and solutions. Where poltergeist activity results from one person's emotional state, the issue needs to be treated with sensitivity and respect. Sometimes a far more sensible alternative to chasing the poltergeist is recommending sound medical assistance.

A GUIDE TO GHOST-HUNTING

If you regularly tune in to the *Most Haunted* TV show, you'll see us using all manner of sophisticated ghost-hunting equipment. There really are some superb ghost-hunting aids on the market these days, and I'd advise you to examine these hi-tech units if you are looking to back up investigation successes with scientific evidence.

However, when starting out as a ghost-hunter you can, if you wish, get away with pretty basic equipment, much of it to be found around the house.

A **torch** is essential and **candles** are useful too because in addition to giving soft light they can detect movements and draughts. Another 'must have' is a **tape recorder** or **Dictaphone**. A useful rule with regard to taping sound is not to leave your recorder running – it's painstaking and ultimately unrewarding to listen back to hours of tape after a ghost-hunting session. Much better to use your tape recorder only when you have asked your ghost a question – such as the classic 'Is anybody there?' Then switch on your recorder and leave it on for two or three minutes and you could get some very good results.

You can get away with an everyday **thermometer** to gauge sudden drops in temperature, but better still is a **laser thermometer**, which detects the temperature at exactly the point its red scan light hits and gives a reading on a handheld gauge.

Tape – such as household masking tape – is useful for taping off areas of activity or windows. A piece of **thread** can also be useful to section off small areas, such as a tabletop.

To assist in monitoring the movement of trigger objects, items that move during poltergeist activity, an upturned **transparent case** can come in handy. Try a plastic fish tank – and I'd recommend an empty one! Putting trigger objects underneath plastic makes for a more scientific examination of item movement because it eradicates the possibility of anything being moved by natural factors, such as draughts or wind.

In the absence of digital recording equipment, something as basic as a piece of **graph paper** at least gives you the opportunity to map out items on a table or in a room before and after a poltergeist haunting.

Dowsing rods are ghost-hunting implements you need to acquire a relationship with, and a feel for, quite literally! In simple terms the rods are two pieces of thin rigid wire, the consistency of a typical Firework Night sparkler and around 18 inches long in each case. Place each rod lightly between the first and second finger of each hand and, with fists clenched and facing away from the body, and elbows slightly bent, hold the rods out horizontally in front of you approximately six inches apart. Try them out in any space, particularly one where a haunting has been reported, and simply ask the rods to give you 'yes' and 'no' answers to questions. I believe you get a 'yes' when the rods cross inwards and a 'no' when they angle away from each other. If you ask if a spirit is in the room you are in and the answer is 'yes', you can then ask the rods to point in the direction of the spirit. Patience and concentration is needed, but in my experience dowsing rods really do work. I don't know *how* they work but my gut feeling is that it's something to do with the power of the mind transmitting itself through the body and into the rods. Ask me for a scientific explanation and I can offer none, but my own personal experience of using rods is both positive and genuine.

If and when you really catch the ghost-hunting bug you might want to invest in some of the incredibly sophisticated pieces of state-of-the-art equipment now on the market. Such is the interest that there are companies such as the British-based Spectral Electronics that now deal exclusively in ghost-hunting aids.

The **Electro-Magnetic Field (EMF) meter** has been used for several years now by ghost-hunters and by paranormal investigators. This hand-held machine, not much bigger than a TV remote control unit, can detect electro-magnetic presence in the fabric of buildings; useful when investigating, for example, regular reported sightings of an apparition in the same place. The latest generation of EMF meters, developed specifically for paranormal investigators, are ingenious because they filter out everyday electrical charges such as mains frequencies. With a pair of normal headphones you can also measure variations in electro-magnetic energies recorded by the meter.

The **Ultra-Sonic Unit** is pretty new on the market. In look and feel it is similar to an EMF meter with a display and an audio connection. Ultra-Sonic Units measure acoustic energies in ultrasound regions at frequencies of 20khz and above, a range of sound that bats and, significantly, dogs can hear, but way beyond normal human hearing. Animals generally seem more sensitive to paranormal activity than we humble humans and devices such as the Ultra-Sonic Unit help us to redress the balance. Previously some ghost-hunters would take dogs on investigations because they seemed to be able to pick up things that humans couldn't. With the head-phone connection you can monitor high-frequency sounds and, if you wish, record them onto your Dictaphone. Some of the more advanced paranormal investigation groups have even developed computer programs that enable users to store and interpret information using sounds recorded through Ultra-Sonic Units. These programs are available as free downloads on the Internet and can display spectrum analysis ranges that show, for example, energies recorded in different frequencies. So Ultra-Sonic Units do so much more than simply replicating the sensitivity of dogs, and the real beauty of them of course is you don't have to take them out for walks!

The **Negative-Ion Detector** is another 21st-century phenomenon. The low-light infrared filming we carry out on *Most Haunted* often shows up orbs, small objects that seem to fly through the air like tiny flying saucers. These orbs are believed to have some relation to high voltage or static electricity, a side effect of which is a surplus of negative ions. You can create your own electro-magnetic field through the old trick of rubbing a balloon against a jumper, creating an energy that allows the balloon to stick to a ceiling. This is the same type of energy picked up by Negative-Ion Detectors, which give out an audible beep to indicate activity.

Interviewing technique is also crucial, despite the availability of modern-day equipment that can make the business of ghost-hunting easier and ultimately more exciting. Investigators of paranormal activity must be prepared to talk to people who have witnessed a haunting when amassing evidence. It is essential therefore to develop an effective interviewing style. Devoting hour upon hour of your own time to ghost stakeouts is all very well, but it is always important to factor in the experiences of other people who have personal accounts to tell of activity in a particular case. It is rather like a detective cracking a criminal case: having first-hand evidence is fine, but to prove your case you need to accumulate witness statements. For these statements to be as effective as possible, like a police detective, you also need to develop a good interviewing technique. Let your subjects do the talking, prompt them with open-ended questions and gently but firmly ask them to stick to the facts of what they have personally seen or heard, not what they have been told by others.

Always record your interviews on a tape recorder or Dictaphone. Ask permission of your subject first of course, and respect their privacy, but recording interviews is important because it enables you to concentrate not only on what is being said, but on the *way* it is being said. Our intuition helps us form an impression of whether someone is speaking sincerely or lying through their teeth. Witnesses' body language will often either give them away or underline their credibility. If you are convinced by the sincerity of your witness the next step is to listen back to the tape and make a full transcript. This is where you, as a detective, must take a sceptical view of the evidence. If a particular witness informs you, for example, that a door in a particular building regularly slams shut for no reason, then look for a logical explanation. Is the activity caused by a through-draught that occurs naturally when another door is opened elsewhere in the house? If a witness reports the smell of tobacco in a particular room at certain times and attributes this to the presence of a pipe-smoking ghost, could it in fact be more to do with temperature changes inducing an odour in paintwork, plaster or old floorboards? Could the sound of ghostly footsteps be nothing more sinister than your neighbours in the house next door, movement in the rooms above or even thermostatically controlled central heating kicking in with a rumble and a thud?

In Tutbury Castle there's a 17th-century costume presented on a shop window-style mannequin that appears to sway entirely on its own. In fact the room where this costume is displayed shares the same old floorboards as the adjoining King's Bedroom at the Castle. Although a partition wall was erected to make one room into two at some stage in the Castle's history, the effect of walking in the King's Bedroom moves the floorboards in the adjoining room and sets the mannequin moving!

Your most reliable witnesses will inevitably be people who live or work in the place where they report paranormal activity. They will be aware of everyday sounds that have a natural cause and will be able to speak to you with greater authority about happenings that are genuinely unusual. The problem with ghost hunts and people whose experiences relate to a location they are not familiar with is that every small sound or movement seems to demand an explanation. It's far better to rely on the witness statements of people who are truly familiar with the place where a ghostly presence is reported. Give particular weight to the statements of those witnesses who stick to the facts of what they have experienced rather than speculating as to the cause. If they tell you they regularly hear footsteps in the cellar followed by a loud bang, but haven't any idea what causes this phenomenon, it's a more telling observation than someone who goes on to speculate that the activity is probably caused by the ghost of an unhappy monk who hanged himself in the

15th century, because Mrs Jones in the village reckons the house was once the site of a monastery…

A **methodical approach** is crucial for ghost-hunting. Sherlock Holmes may be a fictional detective, but he was given a very factual philosophy on detection. When approaching a case he would rule out the impossible and examine what he was left with, as this, he believed, was the truth, however improbable that truth seemed.

I can testify from personal experience to the emotion attached to seeing a ghost at first-hand and the careful analysis I went through afterwards to convince myself of what I had seen. It happened in Derby Gaol, not at dead of night during a low-light ghost hunt, but in the middle of the afternoon in a kitchen when I was on my mobile phone in conversation with a friend. Through the open door of the kitchen I saw a figure, the size of a person and grey as grey, move down one of the old gaol's corridors. Although there was no drop in temperature, I sensed it as well as seeing it. By the time I got to the actual door to the corridor, it had gone.

This experience frightened me, quite a lot. However, when I recovered I then went through the process of ruling out all the naturally occurring things that might have caused its appearance. Although what I saw had a misty appearance, it wasn't smoke, it wasn't steam and it wasn't the reflection of a car's headlights. There's a theory known as 'Standing Wave' that tells us that in certain conditions extractor fans in rooms, corridors and even in computers can give off an odd acoustic effect that creates the impression of something moving fleetingly at the very edge of an individual's vision and prompts terrible feelings of fear and anxiety. However, the grey mass I saw wasn't out of the corner of my eye; it was a full-on experience and I can think of no other explanation than my having witnessed a ghost.

Here is something strange but true: while filming an episode of *Most Haunted* I saw a spoon fly through the air. I wasn't the first person to the errant spoon when it landed and my slowness off the mark on this occasion probably saved me getting my fingers burned! In some instances items subject to poltergeist activity, whether cutlery, coffee cups or other general household objects, have been found to be red hot to the touch. This I put down to the poltergeist energy created in its movement, so approach with care!

Continuing the methodical approach to all things paranormal, it is important to log examples of poltergeist activity for future reference, so always weigh the object that has apparently moved and measure how far it has travelled. This statistical information can help you prove, for example, that items of a certain weight tend to travel a certain distance in a particular room. At the very least it is information you can pass on for others to quantify. Organisations such as the Society for Psychical Research will always be happy to offer assistance provided you have facts and figures to support your questions.

Original artefacts are always good for measuring powers of perception through a simple touching and sensing test. Anyone can try it, though some, inevitably, are more sensitive than others. Here's what you do, in a group if you wish: lay the palms of your hands lightly on an artefact – anything from a sideboard to a sword – and then clear your mind completely. Try to register signals from the item you are touching; then talk about it.

Folklore is the development of history rather than hard historical fact. For example, it may be factually correct that in the Middle Ages a woman leapt to her death from the north tower of a castle after her knight husband returned early from battle to discover her with a lover. The folklore element is the tale passed down through the ages that the apparition of a white lady is seen leaping from the same tower just before midnight, or that a candle will never burn when lit in the room at the top of the tower.

So how, as a ghost-hunter, do you try to bridge the gap between folklore and fact? First, as always, gain permission from the owners of the property you intend to investigate. You may even feel it is sensible to have a member of staff of the haunted building – a curator of the castle for example – present throughout the investigation. At the very least, draw up a written agreement with the owners or trustees of the building that your investigation has been sanctioned. I would then devise experiments suitable to the environment and probably arrange a vigil where at least two people, armed with digital recording equipment, sit at the haunted site and quite literally wait for something to happen. The vigil might take the form of a small séance where you as the ghost-hunter invite spirits to make contact. Although you as the leader of this particular investigation will be fully aware of the folklore surrounding the site in question, it's probably a good idea that others in the vigil party know as little as possible and go into the experiment with few pre-conceptions.

Ensure too that **evidence** collected during the vigil is not contaminated by over-elaboration. If, for example, a member of the party sees the apparition of an old soldier walking through a wall, he should not turn to a colleague and ask: 'Did you see the old soldier walk through the wall?' The best response would be simply to ask: 'Did you see that?' The colleague then replies with a simple 'yes' or 'no', again guarding against over-elaboration that might later be construed as auto-suggestion. Importantly though, both members of the vigil should make a note of the time of the conversation and record exactly what they did or didn't see.

If you see a ghost-hunter seemingly poking himself in the eye in a moment of high excitement during a vigil, don't be alarmed! An interesting theory supported by some in this business is that a ghostly apparition is genuine if, when you press very gently on one eyeball, you see a double image for a split second. If what you are seeing is a hallucination – a product of the mind – apparently you will only see a single image.

If you have a **medium** in your party it is fascinating to record his or her verdict on contacts made during the séance. Afterwards you can check the medium's connections and findings against established historical fact.

My view is that you cannot get closer to history than actually seeing a ghost. Parapsychologists take a different angle. They prefer in the first instance to talk to people who claim to have witnessed paranormal activity rather than attempting to experience the phenomenon themselves.

Whichever approach you choose to take, be as methodical and unemotional as possible. Your body needs to listen and work in a new way, so try to rest as much as possible in the hours before the investigation takes place. You will probably be up all night, so you will need all the energy and awareness you can muster. Don't confuse your body either by treating it to large doses of alcohol or a large spicy dinner before a vigil; eat sensibly and take along snacks that will give a kick to your blood-sugar levels during the night. Remember at around three o'clock in the morning the body goes into a different mode. This is the time when most people die and most people are born, and it is also the stage during all-night vigils that you need to give your body some fuel. Be as healthy as possible in body and spirit and be aware that even something as simple as a common cold can potentially confuse an investigation. Was that the ghostly tolling of a distant bell you just heard, or a buzz in your ears brought about because you blew your nose?

Many people like to take a **psychic** or medium on a ghost hunt. Do *not* tell them where you are going. Drive them to the location yourself, giving nothing away. You then need to measure exactly how accurate the psychic is. This can be done by creating a map of the location and recording the findings of more than one psychic at each point on the map. Alternatively draw up a list of emotive words, such as 'Happy', 'Angry', 'Murder', 'Child', 'Mediaeval' and so on... and ask each psychic to ring the words they feel most appropriate to particular areas of the location. If you discover that more than one psychic logs the same emotions in the same areas, then you are accumulating useful evidence of a haunting.

I believe the vast majority of psychics have an innate ability to see something the rest of us can't detect. It's a gift in the same way as someone who has the God-given talent to play a piano without music. I also know there are some complete charlatans practising as psychics, but I believe in ghosts and I believe in the supernatural, so I have to believe in mediums.

I have a party-piece when visiting, in particular, ancient sites such as castles, which demonstrates powerfully to me the energy that emanates from stone. I have a crystal on a string that I carry around with me and I have shown tens of thousands of people on my ghost walks how an ancient stone's energy can make the crystal swing on the string of its own accord. All I do is hold the piece of string with the crystal attached in one hand, and place the palm of my other hand on the stone. Within seconds the crystal will start to move – without any assistance from me – and I can only explain this as the energy transferring itself through my body, using the power of the mind. The moment I lift my hand from the stone, the crystal's gyrating action slows down and eventually stops. I don't cheat; I don't have to, and I defy anybody to come up with an explanation for this feat that doesn't have a supernatural foundation.

Before you read on, remember that most people who see ghosts aren't frightened when they see them, because the ghosts usually look like real people. The other important thing to remember is that eight out of 10 ghost stories can be accounted for; it's the other two you need to worry about!

So sleep well, and don't have nightmares.

GLOSSARY OF GHOSTLY TERMINOLOGY

Amulet is an item that has the power to stave off ghosts and evil spirits.

Angel is something often mistaken for a ghost, but in fact is a holy and protective messenger shielding us from harm.

Animal ghosts are believed to be the spirits of animals who survive the death process. Many experts in the paranormal acknowledge the existence of animal ghosts and some investigators even believe animals have what is known as a 'collective soul'. This theory supposes that as many as half a dozen animals at one time may share just one soul.

Apparitions are recorded in the earliest pages of history. This mysterious image of a disembodied spirit can be recognised as a human or animal. They are the most rare type of ghost to capture on film. Ghostly human forms are the easiest to fake, especially with the advanced technology of computers. This makes our job even more difficult, as it is almost impossible to prove the existence of apparitions when using photographs. Ghostly apparitions of ships, trains, cars and other inanimate objects have been seen. Some are said to appear to warn of a disaster that is about to happen, while others are thought to guard sacred places. Some apparitions are not seen, they are heard, or felt.

Apport happens when a solid object appears from nowhere, with the assistance of the spirit in the company of a medium.

Astral body is the energy that separates itself from the human form but still maintains the personality and feelings of the individual. Sometimes others will see them during an out-of-body experience (OBE) or a near-death experience (NDE).

Astral plane can be described as a level of awareness in the celestial world with its own standards and occupants.

Atmospheric apparition is a visual imprint of a person that has died left to be replayed on the atmosphere.

Aura is an energy field that surrounds all living things.

Automatic writing occurs when a ghost or spirit takes control of the writer's hand and pens a message.

Banshee is a spirit that appears before a person's death to howl a mourning song and to welcome them into the afterlife. It is also Ireland's most famous ghost. The correct pronunciation of this female spirit's name is 'bean si' and she is said to associate herself with Irish families – particularly if their surname starts with the letter 'O' – and she is more likely to be seen by a third daughter. Her appearance is said to be the portent of death for a family member, announced by crying and wailing during the hours of darkness. The sound is said to be like that of two cats fighting, only much worse. The tragic relative might be thousands of miles away in another country, and the wailing can apparently be heard for several nights in succession until the actual death occurs. The woman herself appears in contrasting ways. Sometimes she is described as a strange-smelling small, ugly hag dressed in rags. At other times she appears as a young and beautiful woman in a green dress, her eyes red and swollen from constant crying. A third type of banshee has also been reported, but it is not clear whether she is young or old, as she has no clear features, with holes where her eyes should be. The common factor linking all three types is very long hair that streams out in the wind. Folklore dictates that when a banshee is disturbed by a mortal person she will not appear again while that generation lives, but will return to haunt future generations.

Bi-location describes the phenomenon where someone can be in two places at the same time.

Birds were at one time believed to be messengers of the dead – when one tapped on a window, it was said to signify that a ghost was looking for another spirit to join it. Certain birds, such as sparrows, larks and storks, were said to transport to earth the souls of people from the Guff, or 'Hall of Souls', in heaven. Other birds, especially crows, were believed to carry the spirits of humans onto the next plane of existence.

Boggart is a word used chiefly in the north of England to describe a particularly nasty type of ghost. Boggarts are said to enjoy crawling into victims' bedrooms at night and pulling the bedclothes off, slapping, pinching and biting people, especially on the feet. In appearance they are said to be truly frightening, with sharp, long and yellowing teeth.

Bogies, like the Irish banshee, are said to make a wailing noise. An unpleasant spirit with a preference for haunting children, the bogie, according to British folklore, is foul-smelling, black, short and hairy with an ugly, grinning face. Perhaps it belongs more to the language of parents, hence the warning: 'Don't be naughty, or the bogie man will get you!' Bogies were once thought to be the most powerful of ghosts, having apparently once served the Devil by doing evil deeds against mankind.

Cats, next to dogs, are the most common form of animal spirits. The ghost cat is believed to have its spooky origin in ancient Egypt where cats were often worshipped, especially at Bubastis, where many thousands of mummified cats have been excavated. Historically the Devil was believed to be able to take the form of a cat, and cats were often thought to be witches' familiars.

Cemetery lights hover over graves after dark as bluish balls of light.

Channelling is a form of spirit possession that occurs with a medium who is communicating with an unseen entity to gain wisdom or gain knowledge of future events.

Clairaudience, a skill claimed by many mediums, is when someone has the ability to hear the voices of ghosts and other sounds that are inaudible to the human ear. These disembodied voices of the dead, or other entities, normally tell of events yet to happen. Many mediums say that they can hear dead relatives passing on information from a place they call 'the Spirit World'.

Clairvoyance is being capable of seeing events in the future or past through the mind's eye. In its simplest form, clairvoyance is to 'see with sight beyond the normal human range of sight'. A clairvoyant can see visions of events that have already happened, are actually happening or are yet to happen.

Clairsentience is, some believe, a basic human instinct finely attuned and polished. If you are clairsentient, you have the ability to feel and know things that have been, are, and are yet to be.

Cold reading is done when a psychic has no prior knowledge of the sitter.

Cold spot is an area in a haunted place where the temperature drops by several degrees. Temperature can also rise in heat by several degrees, indicating the presence of a fire in the past.

Collective apparition occurs when more than one living person sees a ghost or spirit simultaneously.

Collective unconscious is a term to describe a form of analytical psychology developed by Carl Jung. It represents the collective memory of all humanity's past and is held somewhere inside the unconscious mind.

Conjure is an act to summon a spirit to manifest itself for a desired task or to answer questions.

Corpse candle is a term referring to balls of firelight that can be seen to dance above the ground.

Crisis apparition is the vision of someone that will appear during waking hours or in a dream at the moment of a crisis.

Crossroad ghosts have been reported for centuries, and no-one knows quite why. Some researchers maintain that crossroads are more likely to be haunted because of the number of suicide victims buried there. The superstition behind interring the dead at such places lies in the Christian belief that the cross is a form of protection from demons, vampires and other supernatural night creatures. This theory, however, is thrown into doubt when it is considered that excavated human remains pre-dating Christianity have been unearthed near crossroads all over the world.

Deathwatch is a strange turn of phrase connected with a species of beetle known as the deathwatch beetle, which taps on wood. Many believe the beetle can sense the approach of death and taps in acknowledgement of spirits arriving to take the soul to its next destination.

Dogs have been reported in ghost form all over the British Isles. These spectral dogs are said to vary in size and some have been described as small but with extremely large eyes. They can also be white, black, vicious or gentle. The

Lancastrians have a ghost dog known as a Striker; in Wales there is the Gwyllgi, while Derbyshire boasts Rach Hounds and Gabriel's Ghost Hounds.

Doppelganger is a German word to describe a ghost that is the double of a living person. Those who experience seeing their double are said to be heading towards misfortune in the near future. Confusingly, other investigators are adamant that the doppelganger is also an indication of good fortune, though recorded incidences of them being a good omen are rare. People associated with the haunted individual are also reported as having seen the doppelganger at a place where the living counterpart was nowhere near.

Dowsing is the skill of seeking answers and interpreting them through the use of rods or a pendulum. Dowsing is widely used as a simple but effective way of searching for such things as lost coins, water and ghosts. It is also used to conduct geophysical surveys.

Drudes are mature witches or wizards, and reports of this nightmare ghost date from ancient England. The drude is said to be well versed in the art of magic and able to cause a ghost to appear in the dreams and nightmares of their chosen victims.

Duppy is the name given to a well-known West Indian ghost said to be able to walk the earth only between the hours of dusk and cock-crow. The duppy can be summoned from its grave by an act of ceremonial magic to do the bidding of a witch. The ceremony involves mixing blood and rum together with other substances. This concoction is then thrown on the grave of one known to have been an evil person when alive, as the duppy is widely believed to be the personification of evil in a human.

Earthlights are balls of lights or variable patches of lights appearing randomly and with no explanation as to what causes them.

Ectoplasm is a strange substance said to extrude from the sweat glands, mouth, nostrils and genitals of some mediums while in a trance-like state. A solid or vaporous substance, it is produced by a medium during a trance to reach a dead person. Ectoplasm, or teleplasm, is derived from the Greek words *ektos* and *plasma*, meaning exteriorised substance. There are researchers who claim that the substance is similar to pale white tissue paper, cheesecloth, or fine silk strands that all gather together to make a human shape. Others say the substance is like human and animal tissue. Most reports of ectoplasm have been revealed to be hoaxes. Some mediums have gone to the lengths of taking cheesecloth and rigging it to drop from a part of the body (the nose, mouth or ears). Some mediums even swallowed the cheesecloth and then regurgitated it later during the séance.

Ectoplasmic mist will usually show up in a photo as a misty white cloud to indicate the presence of a spirit. The mist is not seen when the picture is taken. These mists can vary in colour from grey and black to red and even green.

Elemental spirit is a rather curious type of ghost said to be a spirit that has never existed in human form. For this reason, occultists insist they are ancient spirits representing Earth, Air, Fire and Water that predate man. Elemental spirits are often associated with haunted stretches of woodland and rivers, mountains and valleys.

Elves are spirits of nature. Spiteful creatures, they are suffering as lost souls trapped between two worlds; not evil enough to go to hell; not quite good enough to be accepted into heaven.

EMF (Electro-Magnetic Field) meter is a device that can pick up electronic and magnetic fields. It can also detect any distortions in the normal electro-magnetic field.

Entity is a term that refers to an intelligent being who is no longer inside their physical body. They have the power to provide information to all individuals who are sensitive to their vibrations.

ESP (Extra Sensory Perception) represents an ability to gather information beyond the five human senses.

EVP (Electrical Voice Phenomenon or Electrical Visual Phenomenon) is a method by which a spirit's voice is detected by means of a recording device. It is also possible to pick up visual images of a known dead person on computer and TV screens, even when they are not switched on.

Exorcism is a religious ceremony where an attempt is made to expel a spirit that may have taken up residence inside a house or a human being. The ceremony usually involves a clergyman such as a priest, often specially trained, who will say prayers and repeat loud exhortations, often burning candles and sprinkling holy water while incense is burned. Exorcism is actually a modern version of the old Christian practice of excommunication – the rite of 'Bell, Book and Candle' – where sinners were eliminated from further entering the faith by a priest who would ring a small bell and slam the Holy Bible shut, often after reading the Malediction. The priest would then extinguish the burning candles. Modern mediums claim to be able to conduct exorcisms without the usual religious trappings by psychically contacting the spirit causing the problems and convincing it to move on to the next spiritual plane of existence. In some cases it is believed that ghosts in need of an exorcism are spirits that have not come to terms with their passing, especially where their demise has been untimely or tragic.

Exorcist is an individual – usually a religious holy man – who is skilled in removing demons from within people or locations.

Extras is a word used to describe faces or whole images of people that mysteriously appear on photographs. There are many reported instances of pictures revealing the image of a long-dead relative, or even someone still alive but living thousands of miles away, when they are developed. In the early days of photography, many of these wispy images were faked, but there are a small number of examples that defy explanation even today.

Fairies are tiny, invisible mythical beings. The pranks they play are sometimes mistaken for the activities of ghosts or poltergeists. Many types of fairies are believed to exist with each one being connected to an element, as in earth (Gnomes), fire (Salamanders), air (Sylphs), and water (Undines), and the colour green is apparently sacred to them. They are said to live in hills, valleys, among the trees and also where there are ancient burial mounds and ancient stone circles.

Family apparition is a ghost that haunts one particular family. When the ghost appears it is an omen that someone in the family is going to die.

Fireball is a Scottish phenomenon. Described as a medium to large sphere, it moves in a smooth and often slow way, most often over stretches of water. Fireballs are thought to be the souls of the departed returning to earth to guide the souls of people who have recently died to the next world.

Galley beggar is an old English ghost referred to as early as 1584 in Reginald Scot's work, *The Discovery of Witchcraft*. This ghost has the appearance of a skeleton and its name is derived from the word 'galley', meaning to frighten or terrify. The classic image is that of a screaming skeleton – head tucked under one arm – encountered on a country road.

Ghosts are different forms of apparitions of deceased human spirits that can appear to any of our five senses. They can be seen as a shadowy human or animal form. They can be heard and may even emit a familiar or offensive odour. They are trapped between worlds.

Ghost buster is a specialist in clearing an area of ghosts, poltergeists, spirits or other haunted activity.

Ghost catcher is a type of wind chime that will clink together as a ghost wisps by.

Ghost hunt describes a conscious effort to search out a known ghost or to visit other places suspected to be haunted.

Ghost-hunter is a person who seeks to find ghosts or haunted places and tries to determine what type of spirit activity is taking place, and why.

Ghost investigation involves going into an area looking for ghosts or hauntings under controlled conditions. Reports are made to document the events. Listing all the reading of the equipment along with time, weather, and temperature as the project unfolds becomes valuable information for the research.

Ghoul is a grotesque, evil spirit with a terrifying face that gains its sustenance by robbing a grave to eat the flesh of the recently deceased. The ghoul was at one time the common word for a ghost in Arabia.

Graveyard ghost is a ghost believed to have special abilities. According to folklore, the first person to be buried in a churchyard was believed to return to guard the site against the Devil. Because this task was so great, a cat or dog was often buried before any human, so it would become the guardian of the dead and remain so until the Crack of Doom.

Gremlins are a recent phenomenon, originating from World War Two in 1939–45 when pilots flying dangerous missions reported seeing strange goblin-like creatures in the aircraft with them. A 'gremlin in the works' is common parlance now for when machinery grinds to a halt.

Grey lady is said to originate from Tudor times. Some say it refers to the ghost of a woman who has been murdered by her lover or one who waits for the return of a loved one. There's another theory that these ghosts represent the Dissolution of the Monasteries, which resulted in the death of many monks and nuns, who would have been dressed in grey habits.

Hallowe'en can be traced back long before the advent of Christianity. Our ancient pagan ancestors celebrated the 'Feast of the Dead' by lighting great bonfires across the country to summon the dead and placate them by offering burnt sacrifices. The Christian Church is thought to have moved the bonfire tradition to 5 November, marking Guy Fawkes's fate, in an attempt to dilute the true meaning of the night. Modern witches still celebrate the night of 31 October by holding feasts and performing magic rituals. According to legend, Satan opens the gates of hell at the stroke of midnight and all spirits of evil are set free to wreak havoc on earth. By cock-crow these spirits must return to hell, where the gates are slammed shut at the first sight of dawn. Any spirit left outside would disintegrate forever.

Haunted chair is an essentially English phenomenon referring to people who have a fondness for a particular armchair coming back as a ghost and being seen in the same chair.

Haunt is the place where the ghost or spirit continues to return. Ghosts usually haunt places and not people.

Haunting is used to describe the repeated display of paranormal activity in a particular area. Some hauntings are thought to be poltergeist energy from a disembodied entity trapped in a certain location or by the energy left behind from a very strong tragic event or accident. Occasionally, hauntings appear to be an intelligent ghost trying to make a connection with someone on the earthly plane to give a message. People can also be haunted, as can any item that may have belonged to someone deceased.

Headless ghosts are the spirits of people whose death occurred because they were beheaded. There is also evidence to suggest that these types of apparitions may be connected to the ancient practice of beheading the corpses of people suspected of being connected in life with witchcraft and sorcery.

Headless horsemen in ghost tradition are believed to be the results of riders who may have been ambushed and decapitated while riding at speed through wooded glades. Another theory is that headless riders are ancient chieftains who lost their heads in battle and still wander the earth in search of their dismembered heads.

Iron is believed to be a sure antidote against all kinds of bad magic and evil spirits.

Lemures is the Roman word given to evil ghosts who return to haunt relatives and friends. Ceremonies to placate these spirits were often held in ancient Rome.

Ley lines are the invisible lines that run between sacred objects or locations.

Luminous body is the faint glow in a dead body to signify a soul's impending departure.

Malevolent entities are angry spirits, often seeking revenge. They sometimes attach themselves to a living being, causing them discomfort and distress. They tend to impose their anger or depressed personality on the human being they possess.

Materialisation is the ability claimed by some mediums to bring into vision a spirit or ghost. One of the first recorded incidents occurred in America in 1860 and was performed by the Fox sisters, founders of modern day spiritualism.

Medium is someone who can communicate with the dead. During a trance state the medium allows the spirit to take over their body so they can deliver a message to the living. The medium does not remember any of this once they come out of the trance. Today the new mediums refer to this as channelling. The big difference is that nowadays the medium remains completely conscious of what he/she says and experiences through the spirit.

NDE (near-death experience) is when a person dies and is revived after a short period of time. The person remembers their death experience and can recall visions of the afterlife, which include ghosts and other paranormal events. Survivors of this experience say it changes their whole outlook on death and they feel as if they can live better lives after this realisation.

Necromancer is a person considered to be a sorcerer or wizard, who has the power to raise the dead and force the spirits to obtain information about the future.

Orbs are globe-shaped lights of energy caught on film, usually during a haunting or other paranormal experience. Orbs are believed to represent the spirit of an individual that has died. They are made up of the energy force that powered their body in life. They may vary in size, colour and density.

Omen is a prediction of a future event.

Oracle is a prophet that can communicate with spirits, ghosts and gods to obtain information.

Ouija Board is a board with cards of numbers – zero to nine – the letters of the alphabet, and the words 'yes', 'no' and 'goodbye' printed on the surface. A glass beaker or wine glass is placed on the table and the consultation can then begin. The board comes with a planchette (a pointer) and once you lightly place your hand on it the pointer will spell out the answers to the questions asked by the players. This 'game' can be dangerous if participants are not fully aware of what they are doing and are not educated in psychic science.

Paranormal is any experience that happens beyond the range of scientific explanation or normal human capabilities, including hauntings, telekinesis, telepathy, clairvoyance, or any other rarity that cannot be justified by the five senses.

Perfumed ghosts manifest themselves in the form of a scent. Many people have experienced smelling the favourite scent of a deceased relative, such as an aunt or grandmother.

Phantom coaches are also known as 'death's messenger', and are apparently seen in silent progress before a death in the family. The horses are always said to be headless and the coaches are described as black and sometimes have the appearance of a hearse. The skeleton-like driver is usually viewed as horrendously ugly, with a fixed grin.

Planchette is a pointer used with an ouija board to communicate with spirits, ghosts, or entities of a higher plane.

Poltergeist is a noisy and sometimes violent spirit. While ghosts haunt and like solitude, poltergeists infest locations and prefer company. The name 'poltergeist' means 'noisy ghost'. Known traits of the poltergeist are banging, thumping, moving objects, levitating, and causing fires. These same results can also be attributed to an unconscious outburst of psychokinesis. More researchers of today feel that much reported poltergeist activity is related to psycho-kinesis rather than a ghost.

Possession is when an evil entity takes over a human body and forces the soul out. This allows the spirit to use the host by exerting its own will. This may totally adjust the host's current personality. Women aged under 20 are most commonly attacked in this way and show clear signs of emotional distress. The discarnate spirit seeks out humans to display emotions of anger, revenge and resentment.

Precognition is the foreknowledge of future events.

Psychic is a person who tunes into phenomena beyond their five senses and has the ability to see or sense the future, present and past. The talents of a psychic include but are not limited to hearing voices, seeing spirits and knowing what might be happening in the future. Unfortunately these gifts have been misinterpreted as mental illness for some. Psychics have also been referred to as seers or sensitives.

Psychokinesis is the ability to move objects using only the power of the mind.

Psychomancy is the ancient art of reading future events through the appearance of ghosts, interpreting what their manifestations to the living might mean.

Purgatory is the place where the souls of the dead must go to be cleansed of all their sins before being allowed into heaven, according to Catholicism.

Reciprocal apparition is an experience where the individual and ghost see and react to one another.

Reincarnation is the belief that once a person dies their soul returns to a new body where it will continue to learn lessons about life and how to reach enlightenment. Many reincarnations may be necessary for the soul to learn and become closer to the goal of perfection.

Retrocognition is the foreknowledge of past events.

Salt, according to ancient customs, is an antidote to all manner of witchcraft and evil spirits. It is said anyone carrying salt in his or her pocket is protected, even against the Devil himself. Placing salt in every corner of rooms in a haunted building is also said to subdue wicked spirits.

Scrying is a form of divination in which an individual stares deeply into an object such as a crystal ball, mirror or flame, in order to see an image that might appear. Such images – usually generated by a spirit – can be symbolic and give answers to a question.

Séance consists of a group of people sitting in a circle holding hands in the hope of contacting the dead. The procedure is conducted by a medium that goes into a trance, as a vehicle for the deceased spirit to take over and communicate with loved ones, sometimes through a spirit guide. Knocking or rapping sounds can also be heard during a séance. The word is of French origin, meaning 'a sitting', and there's no limit to the number of participants, though even numbers apparently get better results.

Sensitive refers to a person who can detect paranormal events beyond the range of their five senses.

Shaman is a medicine man or witch doctor who can communicate with the spirits during a trance and who also possesses the power of healing.

Sixth sense is to have the power of perception in addition to the five senses. It is also a popular term for ESP.

Smudging is a form of cleansing or clearing a spirit from an area by using incense to purify the area.

Spectre is most commonly used now to describe a ghost that is faked or the result of natural factors.

Spirit guide is a heavenly spirit or guardian angel that is present and offers help to the individual to which it is attached. This help may be a simple feeling that comes over the person when they need guidance for a problem or situation. Some people claim they can communicate with their guides at all times.

Spirit photography is usually a photo that contains a face or form believed to be that of a deceased person.

Spiritualism is a belief structure that assumes that spirits and ghosts can communicate with the living.

Supernatural is when an unexplained occurrence take place out of the realm of the known forces of nature. The experience usually involves spirits.

Table-tipping (typology) is a type of communication with the spirit world by using a table. Participants start out with any size table and surround it with a number of people. Everyone places all five fingers lightly on the table. All together the group chants, 'Table up, Table up'. Usually the table will start to quiver or lift to one side. If someone in the group has strong energy the table might rock back and forth or lift off the floor. At this point a question may be asked with a response from the table tapping, once for 'yes' and two for 'no'. If there is a non-believer present the table will probably not move. This type of entertainment can be dangerous and is not recommended to those not skilled in psychic science.

Talisman is a protective charm or amulet said to have the ability to ward off evil.

Telekinesis is where a person can move an object through the power of thought without physical means to move the object.

Telepathy is a method of communication from mind to mind, sometimes across great distances.

Teleportation happens when an object is transported from one location to another by disappearing and then reappearing in a different place.

Time slips occur when the past and present collide at a location.

Trance, a state between being asleep and awake, is where a medium uses his or her body as a channel for waiting spirits to pass messages through to living relatives and friends.

Transmigration is the belief that a soul can move from body to body through the process of reincarnation.

Vassage is a spirit that inhabits a scrying crystal. During a scrying session, the spirit communicates by forming literal or symbolic images.

Vengeful spirits return from the dead to avenge terrible wrongs that have been done to them.

Vortex is a small tornado-shaped image that shows up on pictures when there is a spirit present. Orbs can apparently be seen rotating inside the shaft. Sometimes the vortex is so dense it will cast a shadow. It is believed that the vortex is a means of travel for spirits in the orb form.

Wakes are a noisy ancient custom of watching over the dead while vast amounts of alcohol are consumed. This tradition, especially popular in Ireland, is based on the theory that drinking – as alcohol is a cleanser – helps the spirit of the deceased on its journey to the next world. Music, singing and laughter are encouraged, as it is believed loud noises keep evil spirits at bay.

Warlock is often used to describe a male witch, but this is insulting to many so-called warlocks, as the word has been used in the past to describe a traitor.

White ladies have been seen all over the British Isles, traditionally haunting castles, mansions, halls and even bridges and stretches of water. In ancient times, pagans, to give them a safe passage, apparently sacrificed young women to river gods.

Will-o'-the-Wisp – also known as jack-o-lantern, ignis fatuus, corpse candle and foolish fire – is a ball of flame that floats in mid-air. Such phenomena have also been observed bobbing or dancing just above the ground in yellow and blue flames. These wondrous episodes have been recorded since Roman times. The Native Americans believe them to be a fire spirit warning everyone of danger. The Germans thought the balls of flame were lost or trapped souls that couldn't move on. In Africa some believed that the Will-o'-the-Wisps were witches trying to scare sinners into behaving properly. In Russia, these lights represent the souls of stillborn infants. Throughout Europe when these lights appeared it was thought to be evil spirits that couldn't enter heaven but were not evil enough to be condemned to hell. It would be foolish to follow these strange dancing lights.

Witch is a person – particularly a woman – who practises witchcraft. Most worship nature, but there are different types. Most modern witches would not use their powers for evil, preferring to help human, animal and spiritual awareness. An unwritten law is that witches cannot reveal to anyone what they are or how they practise their art in the belief that silence is power, and power brings knowledge.

Wizard is someone with remarkable abilities and usually proficient in the art of magic. Most male witches prefer this title.

Wraiths are claimed to be the ghost of a person on the edge of death whose appearance should be seen as a warning to the witness that their days are numbered.

PART TWO

THE GHOST
TOUR OF
GREAT BRITAIN

LINCOLNSHIRE

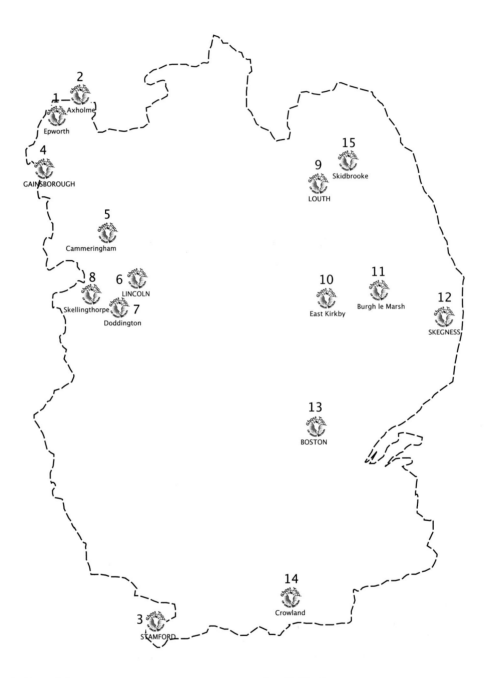

1   Epworth Rectory

2   The Lincolnshire Wetlands

3   The Garden House Hotel, St Martin's, Stamford

4   Marton Church, Gainsborough

5   The Cammeringham Light

6   LINCOLN: Lincoln Cathedral; The Jews House;
                  Browns Restaurant and Pie Shop;
                  Lincoln Castle; The Strugglers Inn.

7   Doddington Hall, Tom Otters Lane

8   Skellingthorpe

9   Thorpe Hall, Louth

10   East Kirkby Airfield

11   Gunby Hall, Burgh le Marsh

12   Skegness Train Station, The Vine Hotel

13   Boston, The Boston Stump

14   The Abbey Hostel Hotel, Crowland

15   Skidbrooke

INTRODUCTION

Lincolnshire is the second largest county in England and is mostly flat land, protected from flooding by the man-made sea defences. The once widespread marshes are now mostly drained. It contains numerous quaint villages, some still with cobbled streets. There are many old buildings with their own ghostly tales, myths and legends, and a few old RAF bases in the county are reputed to be home to former airmen who continue to haunt the grounds, from mere sightings to physical poltergeist activity. There is no better place to start my visit of haunted Lincolnshire than in the centre of Lincoln. Throughout the county there are treasures to be found including one of the original four copies of the Magna Carta, housed in Lincoln Castle, the birthplace of the poet Alfred Tennyson and the former home of Sir Issac Newton. Standing by the dark statue of Alfred Lord Tennyson, one of Lincolnshire's most famous sons, in front of Lincoln Cathedral, I am reminded of one of his haunting poems, *The Ring*, which sets the scene perfectly.

> *My people too were scared with eerie sounds,*
> *A footstep, a low throbbing in the walls,*
> *A noise of falling weights that never fell,*
> *Weird whispers, bells that rang without a hand,*
> *Door handles turn'd when none was at the door,*
> *And bolted doors that open'd of themselves:*
> *And one betwixt the dark and light had seen*
> *Her bending by the cradle of her babe.*

And I remember once that being waked
By noises in the house – and no one near –
I cried for nurse, and felt a gentle hand
Fall on my forehead, and a sudden face
Looked in upon me like a gleam and pass'd
And I was quieted, and slept again.
Or is it some half memory of a dream?

Alfred Lord Tennyson was born in the rectory in Somersby in Lincolnshire in 1809, as his father was rector there. He spent most of his childhood in the rectory and went to school nearby in Louth. He wrote many poems and there were some with ghostly themes like the one above, maybe because, like so many rectories, the one in which his was raised could have actually been haunted.

Lincoln itself is over 2,000 years old, and the traces of its

The statue of Alfred Lord Tennyson, one of Lincoln's most famous sons, with the mediaeval cathedral in the background.

Somersby rectory where Tennyson was born and may well have had ghostly experiences that became the subject of some of his many poems.

Roman builders are still clearly visible in the pattern of streets and ancient fortifications, including remnants of the old city wall, aqueduct and well. The cathedral and the castle leave a fine reminder of Lincoln's Norman heritage, and even though they have both been rebuilt and added to over the years they stand as testimony to the skills of the mediaeval craftsmen. Sixteenth-century and Georgian properties add to the city's architectural heritage. Lincolnshire also has a long military history connected to it and houses RAF stations and former airfield sites, including perhaps one of the most famous bomber command stations, RAF Scampton. There are reports of paranormal activity relating to many of these places, which we will explore in this book.

I have explored Lincolnshire and even spent time here in my youth, and I have spoken to local people who recount tales of strange noises, poltergeist activity and sightings of spiritual beings.

I

LINCOLN CATHEDRAL

This impressive, stone mediaeval cathedral dominates the Lincoln skyline and was originally consecrated in 1092 and was built by Bishop Remigius, a Benedictine monk and supporter of William the Conqueror at the Battle of Hastings in 1066. When it was completed, it was so impressive that the monks believed that the devil would not be able to resist malicious acts towards the building and that he looked upon it with a sour expression. The current building mostly dates

Lincoln Cathedral.

The inside of the cathedral where the Lincoln Imp caused much mayhem.

from the 13th century when it was rebuilt in the Gothic style, but the west front incorporates the surviving part of the original building, and it is possibly the finest mediaeval cathedral in the whole of Europe. It was also a landmark, perched on top of the hill, during the whole of World War Two, for the bomber crews that were stationed at many of the airfields in Lincolnshire.

There are tales of love, murder, saints and sinners linked with the cathedral, and it does have a ghost story: a 17th-century monk in habit with a hood covering his face has been seen here, standing on the cold, stone steps of the cathedral. He turns around and then drifts, seemingly aimless, back through the huge, black door. His identity and the reason for his wandering remains unknown.

There is also a fascinating story associated with the inside of the cathedral of the famous Lincoln Imp. This legend has been told for hundreds of years and there are many versions of it. One such story goes that once a real demon was blown into Lincoln during a tremendous storm. In his curiosity to see what the cathedral had to offer, he slipped inside unnoticed and stayed there, and, as he was one of the devil's creatures, he started causing mayhem, tripping over the bishop and the verger and playing havoc with the angel choir. The guardian angels of the cathedral tried in vain to get the imp to behave until they could stand no more of his bad behaviour. So, when the imp was resting high on one of the pillars next to the east window, the angels turned him into stone. To this day the tiny gargoyle can be seen there, positioned half way up one of the stone pillars inside the cathedral, and it is now one of the most famous myths and legends in the world.

The famous Lincoln Imp, immortalised in stone on one of the huge pillars.

Who knows what
eerie stories lie
hidden within the
cathedral walls?

2

THE JEWS HOUSE

At the bottom of Steep Hill, in the heart of the city of Lincoln, now known as The Jewery, is one of the oldest houses in all of Europe and, of course, it has its fair share or haunted tales and ghostly goings on. The two-storey, 12th-century building, now a very fine restaurant, was originally the home of Solomon of Wallingford, but, unfortunately for him, he was found to be clipping the King's coin and was hanged for his crime and the house was forfeited.

The ancient frontage of the Jews House and the attic window, inside which ghostly footsteps have been heard.

The stone plaque on the Jews House wall.

I have been told there are hauntings that occur on the top floor and in the attic. Inexplicable footsteps have been heard going upstairs on numerous occasions, and with buildings of this age it is certainly possible that spirits could be housed between its old walls, suffering from the loss of loved ones or treacherous deeds so they are unable to move on, or maybe it is the ghost of the Solomon of Wallingford taking residence in the house he was forced to give up.

There is a more intriguing tale from a couple of tourists who took photographs of the building. They took three photos in all, but, when they had them developed, on the second photograph the image of a mysterious knight dressed in armour standing in front of the small door to the house can clearly be seen, surrounded by a strange glow that cannot be explained. There is no known story of a knight attached to this building, but there are many tales of knights linked to Lincoln dating back as far as the 12th century when a group called the Templars was formed to protect pilgrims as they

JEWS COURT

BOOKS

New & Secondhand

The entrance to the Jews Court, which is shrouded in mystery.

travelled to and from the holy land.

Next door is the Jews Court. It is a fine, stone building, but there have been so many alterations over the years it is difficult to date it, and, so far, nothing has been discovered to give proof of its construction date. It is traditionally thought to be the site of a mediaeval synagogue, but its history is still largely a mystery.

As with many old buildings, there is a gruesome tale that I know of relating to it, although there may be many more unheard tales. A little boy was thrown down a well and drowned, but the reasons behind what seems to be a cruel and vicious act remain untold. Many years later his body was found, and it is said that he still haunts the courtyard of the Jews Court to this day.

3

BROWNS RESTAURANT
AND PIE SHOP

Also situated on Steep Hill, Browns Restaurant is a very old and atmospheric building and who knows what events have happened here over the years that it has been standing.

Browns Restaurant, the home of an active poltergeist.

During my tour I met Sandy, the proprietor, who has been here for 15 years. He suggests the building houses a troubled spirit person and there have been many examples of paranormal activity and mysterious happenings in his time here that have no normal explanation. Simple things like boxes and pictures have moved, and people who have been in the main restaurant have actually seen objects moving. A set of stone steps lead down to the dark, dimly lit basement of the building where further suspected supernatural activity has occurred.

A more sinister story was told to me by Sandy that was far more terrifying for him that the simple movement of objects. A few years ago he was cooking alone in the old kitchens when he heard a loud banging emanating from downstairs. He ventured down into the basement to investigate the cause of the noise, but he could not find anything down there to explain it. When he returned to the kitchen he saw that one of the sharp kitchen knives was sticking, point first, into the floor wavering backwards and forwards. There was nothing in the kitchen that could have caused the knife to fall, and it seemed that unseen hands had thrown it, as there was no one else around that could possibly have done it. The knife had been left on the bench about 4ft high, and it cannot be explained how it can simply drop off the bench and stick into the floor.

These stories of the physical movement of items all suggest there is a poltergeist at work. This is the explanation believed by Sandy and his co-workers, and they have continued to call him Humphrey, the name inherited from a previous landlord, but no one knows who this person was or why he still resides in the building.

The basement of
this old building
is the site of
much paranormal
activity.

4

LINCOLN CASTLE

Two years after the Battle of Hastings, in 1068, William the Conqueror began building Lincoln Castle. To enlarge the site, on top of an old Roman hill fort, 166 Saxon houses were demolished, and it is one of only two castles in Britain built with two mottes. The castle was the focus of several military battles during the reign of King Stephen and King John and was besieged during the Baron's War in the early 13th

The last view for condemned felons before public execution.

century. The buildings that remain within the castle today are from its later use as a prison and court. The prison is no longer in use and can be visited. At the western end of the castle is an ivy-clad building built in 1826 as the assize courts. These are still used today as Lincoln's Crown Courts. Each county in England and Wales held assize courts at least twice a year. Criminal and civil cases were referred upwards from the quarter sessions courts to the assizes, and were heard by royal justices. Many of the Lincoln assizes took place in March and July, but if large numbers of convicts were to be tried an additional session could be arranged, which would often be in December.

There has been a prison in the castle ever since its earliest days, and various buildings were used to house the prisoners. The front portion of the remaining prison building was built in 1787, designed by Carr of York. It provided accommodation for debtors and felons alike, plus living quarters for the governor and his family.

The 18th-century prison inside the castle walls.

There are numerous tales of hauntings within the old walls of this ancient castle.

In 1844 a wing used as the felon's prison was demolished. A new wing was added and a corridor, which incorporated the chapel, linked the two. The work was completed in 1848, and the felons were housed in the new wing at the rear, women at one side, men at the other.

In 1849 the separate system was adopted, and prisoners were kept isolated in their cells, only leaving them for exercise and to go to the chapel for religious services. Whenever they left their cells, the men wore a special cap that had a peak which covered the face. Holes were cut out of the peak so they could see where they were going but could not see the face of any other prisoner. The women wore heavy veils to hide their faces. For exercise they walked together in a circle holding a rope knotted at intervals. Each prisoner had to hold a knot, which were spaced far enough apart to stop them whispering to the next prisoner.

Inside the castle walls many men and women were imprisoned.

The red-brick building still in the castle grounds was formerly part of the women's section of the prison, and part of the chapel, the exercise yard and another older part of the prison can still be seen. The ghost of a White Lady is active here, and she can still be seen gliding around the building as she appears before visitors when conditions are right. There

The sinister coffin-shaped pews of the prison chapel.

is no story to explain who she is, but the tale may be connected to the women's prison she haunts. Maybe she is a tormented soul who died under tragic circumstances and cannot leave this atmosphere. No one is sure, but certain ghosts, I believe, are no more than a recording and they are not actually there, and I think this could be the case here.

Usually this type of spectral occurrence happens because the person died under traumatic and premature conditions; murders, suicides, executions or battles. I believe because their time hadn't come that the actual recording just before their death can, for want of a better word, be emblazoned or recorded into the fabric of the wall of the building, and the stone, the bricks, the mortar, and possibly even the soil hold this information, and then for some reason we see that recording again just as if someone has pressed the replay button of a video player, which can be quite terrifying for

Maybe not such a warm welcome for visitors in the past.

those who witness such things. It is seen time and time again in the exact same position that the person was in at the time of their death, so if they appear headless or legless it is because the building has changed, for example if they appear headless the ceiling is perhaps lower than it was at the time of death or if the floor was higher this would, of course, have cut them off at the knee, making them appear legless. I am just left wondering what tragic event could possibly have occurred to this White Lady of Lincoln prison.

In Britain hanging was the principal form of execution from Anglo-Saxon times until the death penalty was abolished in 1964, and up until 1816 the executions in Lincoln would take place on the back of a wagon pulled by a horse. The horse drew the wagon away and the condemned person was left swinging in the breeze. But after this date all public executions in Lincoln took place at the top of Cobb Hall. A defensive tower built in around the 13th century, Cobb Hall is a horseshoe-shaped

building at the north-east corner, which was one of the buildings to serve as the castle prison for many centuries. The county gallows were moved here in 1817, and its roof was used for public hangings until 1868.

While at the castle, I followed in the footsteps of all the accused who had to take the steps on their last journey before being publicly executed on Cobb Hall roof. I climbed up the same narrow, stone stairs, and I was overcome with an eerie feeling as I reached the battlements where the executions took place; you cannot deny the dark and overbearing atmosphere of this place. On top of the battlements, looking out on the beautiful Lincoln Cathedral, I looked at the same view that would have been their last before the execution took place above the spectators below.

These condemned people were hanged on what was called 'the new drop', a wooden platform with a trapdoor. This is still preserved and some of the original scaffold fittings that secured the trap door can still be seem as a gruesome reminder of the events that occurred here in the past: the deaths of criminals, murderers and possibly even the deaths of inno-cent men and women.

Thirty-five men and three women were hanged here as a vast crowd of people looked up from below. Hangings in the past

The wooden structure in which a condemned criminal would stand before execution in the castle grounds.

The prison and exercise yard where convicts would walk around, holding a rope so far apart that they were unable to speak to anyone else.

were often carried out in front of spectators as a macabre form of entertainment, and the gallows would be at least 10 feet high so that they could be seen above the battlements.

The executioners would stand and entertain the crowd, reading psalms, a prayer and, of course, the last will and testament, the accused stating whether they were either innocent or guilty, although it made little difference to the outcome. A white cap would then be pulled down over their face, and the executioner would pull a lever and the fate of the felons would be sealed.

The last execution to take place here was in 1859. After that, all executions took place inside the new prison buildings, within the grounds. The dulcet tones of a death bell would be heard and a black flag, the traditional colour to symbolise death, would be raised from above the prison gates to signify that a person was hanging.

It is not surprising that on many occasions, when the wind is howling, people can still hear the ghostly footsteps padding up the stairs to the top of the battlements, and they also hear the creaking of the lever and the slam of the door as the trapdoor swings open.

For the first time in my life I visited the inside of a prison chapel and the pulpit. Here, in this sombre and atmospheric room, before an execution took place the condemned person would have pride of place in front of the congregation on a huge wooden structure, standing in front of an upright, open coffin, which would probably have been the one they had made in prison the week before their execution. Standing in that same spot, I cannot help but feel on edge. They were then taken out of the chapel and executed. In this chapel the pews are very interesting, and slightly disturbing, as they are coffin shaped, which, it is said, was done on purpose by the prisoners who made them as a rather solemn reminder that the only time they would leave this place would be in a coffin.

Another view of the prison within the castle grounds.

5

THE STRUGGLERS INN

The Strugglers Inn in Westgate in the centre of Lincoln is so called because it is in view of the castle and an area where public executions took place. It has also been said that victims would be seen struggling, fully aware of their fate, while being taken from the court into the castle for execution at the gallows near Cuthbert's Yard on Burton Road. It was originally the Struggler Beer shop, the addition of the 's' being quite new.

The famous Lincolnshire executioner William Marwood, who was also a shoemaker and was proud to proclaim his profession as he carried out his grim work with responsibility, introduced the 'long drop' after much thought and experimentation. This new idea meant that death was caused by the neck being broken rather than by asphyxiation, which could cause men and women to struggle for up to a quarter of an hour before they finally expired, much convulsed.

The ghost story at this three-storey pub involves a Norton Disney poacher called William Clark who was a regular at the pub. He was a horrible man and a bully who carried a stick wherever he went to beat anyone that dared to annoy him. One night Clark was drinking in the Smugglers when the bar went suddenly quiet. Clark turned round to find two policemen there to arrest him for the murder of a gamekeeper, who was shot in the legs and subsequently died

The Strugglers Inn, haunted by the ghost of William Clark's dog.

from gangrene. He tried to fight them off with his stick but had no success as they retaliated with truncheons and ultimately carried out his unconscious, beaten body to the gaol. He had shot the gamekeeper while out poaching. William Clark was tried and hanged for his murder. He was the last person to be hanged at the prison in 1877 and there is a small gravestone marked WC 1877 for him in the grounds of Lincoln Castle.

The ghost story doesn't concern William it concerns his dog. Clark was followed everywhere he went by his faithful lurcher, and the dog was often subjected to beatings from Clark's stick and was thin and scarred along its back. The dog was terrified, and every time Clark looked at him the dog would yelp and cry out in fear. Once Clark was arrested the dog had nowhere to go and would wander round the castle walls and scratch on the door of the pub as if looking for his master. The landlord would chase the dog away, and it only survived because the landlord's wife would throw out scraps to it, unbeknown to her husband. On the day of his master's execution the dog was seen crying and whimpering. By then executions were no longer carried out publicly, but it was as if the dog was watching exactly what was happening. Just before seven o'clock the lurcher went rigid and let out the most horrendous howl, which signified to everyone around that William Clark was dead. After this eerie incident, the dog became a celebrity in the Smugglers and was suddenly welcomed in by the landlord as people would travel for miles to see Clark's dog. The dog became thin and miserable without his master and eventually died, but the landlord, not wanting to lose his celebrity, had it stuffed and mounted and displayed it on the bar for many years. Now, on cold and windy nights, many of the pubs regulars, while standing at the bar, can sense a large dog brush past their legs, and scratching and whining is often heard. Some have even seen the outline of the skinny lurcher sitting underneath the bar, as it tilts its head back and lets out a blood curdling, mournful howl.

A sign depicting the last struggle of a condemned man, after which the inn was named.

6

SKEGNESS TRAIN STATION

The railway came to Skegness in 1873 and from then on the town really began to grow. At first there was only a single line, but in around 1900 it was made a double track and continued to be developed into the station we see here today.

The ghost story connected with this station is a much more recent tale from the 1970s when a young lad called Mark spent many hours trainspotting on this station. Most of his family worked for British Rail so he knew a lot of people there and had a great interest in trains, and he used to sit on the empty trains to do his homework.

A view of platform six where an old lady was seen on board a train then vanished into thin air.

One winters' afternoon he was sitting on the Shrewsbury Excursion Train, which would be in the station for three hours before it left, and it was on platform six. The station was quiet as the next train was not due to arrive for a further two hours. He was sitting in an empty carriage doing his homework when he heard a noise in the corridor and got up to see what or who it was. He stepped into the narrow corridor and to his great surprise saw an old lady wearing a very old fashioned purple dress.

She turned to face him and had a very drawn and haggered face, old and tired, and she was standing and scanning the train from side to side looking very bewildered. He went up to her and asked where she was going, but she didn't reply, and if she was an apparition she is unlikely to have known he was there.

He turned away for a second, looking back down the carriage to see if anyone else was around, then he looked back, and in that split second the lady had vanished; whatever had been there had completely disappeared. No athletic person could have disappeared as quickly as that, so she can't possibly have run into another carriage or off the train, which left the boy confused and frightened by what he had seen.

Mark hurriedly got off the train, looking for an explanation, and walked up and down the platform searching for the old lady, but she was nowhere to be seen, and the departure gates were still firmly locked, adding to his unease. There was no way she could have gotten off the platform without Mark seeing her, and to this day Mark still isn't really sure what he saw on that train on platform six. Was it a ghost or not? There seems to be no ordinary explanation so what else could it have been?

7

THE VINE HOTEL

This red-brick building, set in impressive gardens, almost in the middle of Skegness, was an old inn and dates back to the 1600s, and certainly as far back as 1770, and is reputedly one of the oldest in Skegness. This was the haunt of the Skegness smugglers, and there are stories abound of ghosts and murders that took place, which is no surprise in a building so old that has seen much history.

The cupboard in the hotel reception where the skeleton of an unfortunate murder victim was found.

As I walked through the large wooden doors into the hallway I was immediately drawn to the display cabinet within the wall, and a disturbing ghost story concerning it is still told here. In the early part of the last century, part of an interior wall was opened up to put the display cabinet in. The builders began to knock out the bricks, and to their horror they found a skeleton in the wall, which had been completely bricked up. No one had any idea who or what the person could possibly be or how they ended up bricked up within the walls of this building. The skeleton was removed and examined further, and it was determined that this poor soul had been a male, and remarkably it still had on part of a blue uniform. On careful inspection of the buttons from the uniform, it was concluded that the skeleton was a long dead member of the Customs and Excise, but this still didn't answer the question, what had happened to him and what was he doing here?

Due to the close proximity of the sea, the revenue man must have been at the Vine investigating smugglers. There are many tales told of smugglers and their contraband associated with costal towns from over the years and there are often murder stories connected with these disreputable characters. The 19th-century smugglers on the Lincolnshire coast favoured tobacco. His investigations at the Vine must have been fruitful as it was a favoured place for smugglers, and when they realised they were caught these despicable men murdered him and to hide what they had done they buried him in the wall. This gruesome death seems to have left an active spirit, maybe because he was denied a dignified burial or because of the circumstances in which his life was taken from him, so suddenly and unfairly, and it is said that he still roams around the hotel. Many members of staff have seen this unearthly manifestation drifting along the corridors and in and out of rooms, and he has also been seen upstairs, and it seems that he has one particular bedroom that he haunts frequently.

Up a flight of stairs and along a close corridor is the suspected bedroom: room number eight. It makes perfect

The Vine Hotel, where a murdered revenue man still haunts the rooms and corridors.

sense that he would appear here as the room is positioned directly above the make-shift grave that was created for him in the wall below. People have stayed in this room, and on occasions they have gone down to reception before breakfast after a restless nights sleep and, strangely calm, they have asked if there have been experiences reported of a man in 18th-century uniform standing in the bedroom, staring at sleeping occupants, not sure if their confused semi-conscious minds have just been playing tricks on them. Many eye witnesses have reported similar experiences, but the man always just disappears.

There are other accounts of activity occurring near to the Vine, which can only be described as paranormal, relating to a tale of murder retold in this area that begins in the grand lounge of the hotel. This stunning room, with a substantial dark wood beamed ceiling and a fantastic inglenook fireplace with deep, blood-red walls, was a well-known and popular hostelry in the 1860s, and the murder took place not far away. This unlawful killing was committed by a man more accustomed to saving life than taking it: Samuel Moody was a part-time fisherman and a member of the lifeboat at Skegness.

Not unusually, Samuel was out with two friends at the Vine. They spent seven hours drinking there and, in various stages of inebriation, they left in the early hours of the morning and set off back, into the darkness and cold, towards Skegness.

They stopped at a place called Smiths Corner to talk before each of them went their separate ways back to their homes. David Howard was the first to leave the group, and he continued his journey home alone, leaving the other two, Samuel Moody and Eleisha Linn, talking in the moonlight. They chatted for a long time, and they seemed to be quite friendly, which was a bit strange as they had a difficult, love-hate relationship, often arguing and fighting, although it never went any further than this and would always be forgotten the next time they met up. It isn't known what the conversation was about, but, whatever it was, the events that followed must have been fuelled by rage.

Eventually, one of the two went home, and he made his way along the streets until he arrived at his house and got into his bed. But the other one was not so fortunate, he never got there, his journey home that night was the last he would ever make. The following afternoon an 11-year-old boy was left distraught by the sight of the body of Eleisha Linn, which he found lying in a dyke at Smiths Corner. The state of his body showed that he had been dragged through a hedge and dropped into the dyke, his body left lying partly submerged in the water.

The events that unfolded were unbelievable for two men that had considered themselves to be friends. The conversation had escalated to fighting and got out of hand, and, with no one around to stop them, anger had taken over. Unfortunately for Eleisha, he had a very thin skull, and Moody had hit him over the head with such force that he fractured his skull. He was unconscious but still alive, but, not knowing what else to do, Moody dragged him into the water where he later drowned.

Moody was found at home still wet through and with a large cut on the side of his face; it was obvious that he was responsible, and he was immediately arrested and tried for murder, where the whole sorry story was recounted. He claimed he had acted in self defence, but he was unable to explain why Eleisha had been dropped into the water and why he had drowned. Why had a member of the lifeboat team allowed a man to die rather than trying to save his life? And why had he then fled the scene? His weak excuse was that he couldn't remember any of it because he was drunk.

A plea of leniency was asked for, it was his best hope, and somehow Samuel Moody was only sentenced to manslaughter instead of murder. He spent only 15 years in prison for his crime. The horrible events of that night have left Eleisha Linn in turmoil, and he stays in this atmosphere, still roaming around Smiths Corner in the early hours, on quiet, dark nights, as if looking for Moody, to this very day.

To add to the plethora of ghostly goings on associated with the Vine is a haunting tale associated with one of its former tenants, Alfred Lord Tennyson. While in the garden, he wrote *Come into the Garden* sitting under a tree there.

The door leading into the lounge where Eleisha Linn had his last drink before his last ever journey home.

The remaining stump of the tree under which Tennyson wrote one of his poems, in the grounds where his ghost has been seen.

Come into the garden, Maud,
For the black bat, night, has flown,
Come into the garden, Maud,
I am here at the gate alone;
And the woodbine spices are wafted abroad,
And the musk of the rose is blown.
For a breeze of morning moves,
And the planet of Love is on high,
Beginning to faint in the light that she loves
On a bed of daffodil sky,
To faint in the light of the sun she loves,
To faint in his light, and to die.

The tree is still there but is now nothing more than a stump. On frequent occasions many of the staff say they have seen an old man with a white beard walking through the gardens, accompanied by two large dogs, and they believe it to be the ghost of Tennyson haunting his former residence.

8

BOSTON

Boston is an historic market town dwarfed by the Boston Stump, which is the tower of St Botolph's Church, and the name Boston could possibly be a corruption of Botolph's Town. Spooky's Body Piercing Shop, in the shadow of the Boston stump, is an old 16th-century timber-framed, black and white building, and it is so old that it was here when the plague came to Boston in 1585, one of several major occurrences of this dreaded disease in the town, through the promiscuous deeds of one of its former residents. It is believed it came to Boston because of a beautiful woman by the name of Sarah Preston. She was married to a Boston merchant who was years older than her, but she had an insatiable appetite for young men. So, whenever her husband left she would contact these younger men. On this occasion her husband left on a boat from Boston on a business trip to King's Lynn, and no sooner was he out the door that she immediately started writing to some of her favourite suitors to tell them to visit her.

She was sitting upstairs writing when she heard the sound of gravel being thrown at her window, so she looked down to find a young man waiting for her at the door. It was a friend of a friend who had been told to visit, and she let him in and spent the night with him. He left the following morning before she awoke, but unbeknown to her he had been infected by the

A wood cut taken from a mediaevel manuscript depicting an unfortunate victim of the Black Death.

terrible and much feared plague, the Black Death, before he had arrived at her door, which was transmitted by the fleas carried by black rats and was highly infectious.

Soon after, she started to develop some of the hideous symptoms; the results of the infection were grisly. Hideous swellings developed before bursting and blood would be coughed up from the infected lungs, and death usually occurred within one week of infection. She ran out into the middle of the town in despair and delirium, screaming that the plague had come to Boston. Because of her actions, 460 people died in Boston and are buried in plague pits around the town that were set up to deal with the dead.

There are spine-chilling stories of the undead and the living dead that originate from the days of the Black Death. Tales are ripe of people being buried alive because one of the symptoms of the plague was a deep sleep, or a coma, before death. As soon as people were believed to be dead they were taken out of the house and buried as quickly as possible. The plague generated great fear among the people, and because of their eagerness to remove the dead there are disturbing reports here in some of the graveyards of hands appearing out of the soil and of people who were standing around the coffin, all quiet, and then all of a sudden the lid of the coffin started to lift and the person, still alive, started to climb out of it, terrifying the mourners.

9

THE BOSTON STUMP

The Boston Stump measures 272ft high and is part of the 14th-century St Botolph's Church. The stone used in the construction is from nearby Barnack. On a clear day Lincoln Cathedral, 32 miles to the north, can be seen from the balcony of the church tower.

Views of St Botolph's Church and the 272ft Boston Stump, the scene of several suicides since its construction in the 15th century.

Work began in 1309 on the chancel and moved westward, and later, possibly mid-15th century, the immense tower was added. The buttress on the south-west corner of the tower has been used for keeping a record of the heights and dates of flooding.

I climbed to the top via a spiral staircase as the wind thundered behind me, taking each step one at a time up the cold, echoing tower. Halfway up is a lookout, and as the wind howled around me I looked out over the edge to Lincoln, spread out below me. The story behind the strange loud howling of the wind goes back to the founding of a monastery on the site where the stump is now by Saint Botolph in around 654AD. On frequent occasions he relentlessly preached sermons from here to the devil. The devil could do nothing about his preaching and his frustration grew. It is said the wind that still howls round the stump is reported to be the devil huffing and puffing in exasperation as he could do nothing about the incessant preaching here.

Another legend connected with the tower is that of a young woman who has been seen dressed in white. This woman appears every autumn, throwing herself off the tower, plummeting down very quickly and hitting the ground, then she vanishes on impact. Some say that reports of this ghost go as far back as the 17th century, and some even say that it is the ghost of Sarah Preston, who was so distraught for bringing the plague to the town that she threw herself from the tower, unable to deal with the guilt. Up on the tower there are etchings in the stone dating back as far as 1789, which is a reminder of how old the tower is and of the huge number of events that could have taken place here.

In the main part of the church I heard another ghostly tale from the organist who has seen a ghostly apparition walking along the central part of the aisle when there is only him there. He doesn't know of the origins of this person and possible explanations for it have not been found. It is easy for people to make up ghost stories and on a lot of occasions rational explanations can be found for them, but they say he is a most down to earth and reliable person who would definitely not have made it up.

10

ST BOTOLPH'S CHURCH,
SKIDBROOKE

St Botolph's Church in Skidbrooke is a lovely building but is now redundant and has seen much better times.

Tales of hooded monks being seen, strange sounds from all around, unearthly beings and strange stories abound, which is not surprising as the location is so remote and can be quite eerie.

Inside the church, near where the altar was, is a tomb and there are two grave slabs to one side of the inside of the church, which appear to have some relevance to the Knights Templar.

The inside of St Botolph's Church, where hooded monks have been witnessed.

II
SKELLINGTHORPE

In 1693 Henry Stone of Skellingthorpe was buried in a huge tombstone in a graveyard beside another of Lincoln's old stone churches. The tombstone can still be seen there, guarded by sturdy iron railings. Before he died he insisted his grave be placed as close to the wall of the churchyard as possible, away from any trees in the graveyard, but this request was not quite as strange as it seems. The very good

Skellingthorpe Church and graveyard, haunted by the faithful dog of Henry Stone.

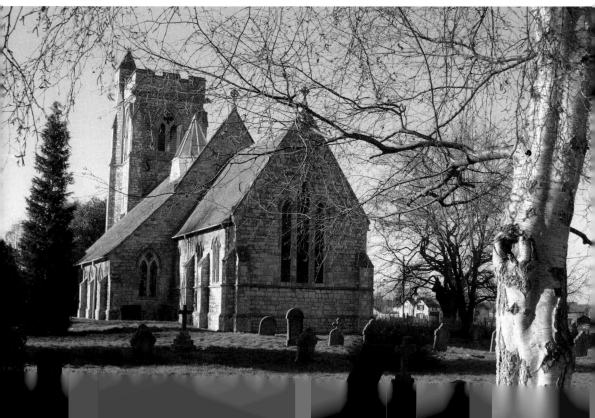

The tomb of Henry Stone close to the graveyard wall so he could be buried next to his dog.

reason for this is that he wanted his dog to be buried next to his grave as he had saved his life. In 1690 Henry was out for a walk with his faithful dog when a violent thunderstorm arose. Henry and the dog took shelter under a large oak tree, but on three occasions the dog grabbed hastily at Henry's hand with his mouth and pulled him away from the tree. Henry kept going back to take shelter there. Then, on the fourth attempt, the dog dragged him anxiously away from the tree again. Then suddenly a bolt of lightening struck the tree, and it exploded and crashed to the ground, killing a pheasant that had taken shelter there. If it had not been for the actions of the dog, Henry would almost certainly have died there. Henry was so thankful that he commissioned a painting of the oak tree, the dog and the pheasant, and this is still on show in the blue drawing room of Doddington Hall.

The dog outlived Henry, and when it died it was buried just on the other side of Henry's tomb, outside the graveyard on the other side of the wall, as he had requested. Unfortunately, the whole area has now been concreted over and there is no monument or stone erected in memory of that faithful dog, but on many occasions people walking past here with their own dogs say they have seen a large, white dog with black patches, just like the one in the painting, sitting panting by the side of Henry's grave. The dog does not come when called or react to passers by, then on second glance the dog has always vanished.

I 2

TOM OTTERS LANE

The B1190, now known as Tom Otters Lane, is a busy stretch of road that joins Doddington and Saxilby in Lincolnshire. The same road existed, although its appearance would have been somewhat different, in 1806 when a Nottinghamshire Navvy called Tom Otter had an affair with a girl called Mary Kirkham, which resulted in her getting pregnant.

In times gone by it was unacceptable for unmarried girls to have children, and as the authorities were unaware at that time that Tom was already married and that Mary had been his mistress they forced him to marry the girl, which would mean he would have to pay maintenance to both wives and his child. The wedding was attended by two parish constables to make sure that it took place as there was something about Tom that they just didn't trust. But he did go through with it even though he wasn't keen on the idea, to say the least.

The following day the two of them set out for Lincoln, Tom still raging from the enforced marriage. Tragically this anger got the better of Tom. He hadn't wanted the marriage, and so Mary never made it to Lincoln. Her body was found the following morning, on this road, and she had been battered to death by a hedge post. Evil Tom Otter was arrested and taken to Lincoln prison, and he was tried and sentenced to hang for murder after an account of events was recalled, convincingly

An example of a gibbet post similar to the one Tom Otter's decaying body would have been hung from after the callous murder of Mary Kirkham.

and graphically, by a supposed eye-witness, who, it was claimed, was also the local peeping tom. Part of his sentence, because he had been convicted of such a heinous crime, was that he be gibbeted near to the scene of the crime. This made it clear to everyone the severity of the crime, and the horrific nature of the punishment was to act as a deterrent and differentiate him from people being hanged for lesser crimes like poaching or burglary.

Gibbeting meant that the body was hung in a metal cage for many years and the felon was left to rot in it, hanging from a huge wooden structure to raise them high off the ground in full view of passers by.

Just as today, everyone in those days craved a decent burial. But, of course, if a body is hung up in a metal cage for many years it couldn't possibly remain whole; parts of the body would start to drop off as the body began to decompose and would be subject to attacks from birds and the like. So being gibbeted meant you wouldn't get that decent burial, and Tom Otter became outraged by what was going to happen to him.

In a vain attempt to alter his fate, he prevented the blacksmith from making his 'final suit', the iron cage his body would be strung up in, by becoming extremely violent. The cage was made all the same, but it wasn't big enough, and Otter had to be crammed into it after he had been hanged. He was raised 30ft high in the air, suspended from a sturdy wooden frame, and was left to be pecked at by the crows.

When the body started to decompose and the flesh started to fall from the jaw bone, it was reported that a blue tit nested inside Tom Otter's mouth and had its young there, and a poem was composed to tell this tale:

Nine tongues within one head,
The tenth went out to seek for bread,
To feed the living within the dead.

For 44 years Tom Otter's body stayed in the iron cage, until in 1850 it was eventually blown down with the gibbet post in a terrible storm. His remains were buried beneath the post, and parts of the gibbet cage are still on display in Doddington Hall. Tom Otter did not leave this place; there are stories abound of him reappearing on many occasions. He is said to have tormented the eye-witness whose account lead to his conviction, particularly on the anniversary of the fateful night. The witness lived in fear of this evil spirit but did not reveal his torment to anyone until he was on his deathbed. People also say that anyone brave enough to walk along the B1190 at night, when the wind is howling, can still hear the creaking of the gibbet cage and the rattling of the chains that held Tom Otter's body all those years ago. There are also tales of him haunting the Sun Inn nearby where his trial took place. Another strange and inexplicable event is also recorded as occurring at the Sun Inn in connection with the ghastly deeds of Tom Otter. The old piece of blood-stained wood that Tom Otter used to kill his innocent wife was purchased by the landlord of the inn because of the huge amount of interest that the murder had generated. He saw it as a showpiece to draw in customers, and it turned out to be a very wise investment. People travelled for miles to see the gibbet where Tom Otter's body was hung up and then completed the macabre tour with a viewing of the murder weapon.

On the first anniversary of the death of Mary Kirkham the hedge stake mysteriously disappeared from the shelf. The landlord went out to the gibbet and to his astonishment he made the chilling discovery of the stake dripping with what seemed to be fresh blood. The same thing happened again the following year, and again the stake was found near the decaying body of Tom Otter with blood dripping from it.

On the third anniversary the landlord organised a watch over the hedge stake through the night, but one by one they fell asleep and once again when they awoke the hedge stake was by the gibbet, dripping with fresh blood. The final fate of the hedge stake remains a mystery as it eventually disappeared without a trace, but many people believe that it was the spirit of Tom Otter picking up the stake each time and who knows where or when it may appear again.

13

DODDINGTON HALL

Doddington Hall is situated between Skellingthorpe and Tom Otters Lane. This beautiful late Elizabethan mansion was completed in 1600 by Robert Smythson for Thomas Taylor, a registrar to the Bishop of Lincoln, and appears today as it did on completion, with walled gardens, huge windows, turrets and a gatehouse, although the interior decoration has changed over the years. An extensive redesign of the interior was carried out by John Delaval of Seaton Delaval when he took over the hall in 1749, but the exterior has not changed at all since it was first built.

In 1830 the hall changed hands again when it was inherited by George Jarvis from his ladyfriend Sarah Gunman of the family of Captain Christopher Gunman, who in the 17th century played an important part in the redevelopment and renewal of the navy. The current owners are direct descendants of George Jarvis. The house is now full of fascinating textiles, porcelain, furniture and family portraits, including that of Henry Stone's dog above the mantelpiece in the blue drawing room. Over the years different people from different families have taken on the upkeep of the hall; however, it seems that there are some slightly more long-term residents here from another dimension.

Claims have been made that the hall is haunted by a screaming lady who, every autumn, is seen throwing herself

Doddington Hall and gardens, where visitors have felt a sense of unease as they walk past the site of the death of a woman after she committed suicide by jumping from the roof.

The entrance to this grand hall and gardens, where a ghostly woman has appeared to greet the brides.

from the roof of the building, plunging into the garden below. People have also reported feelings of distress and unease as they walk across the ground where she landed after her fatal descent. It is said that she jumped off the roof in the 18th century to avoid the local squire, who was making a pass at her in the hall, quite clearly unhappy at his advances. Although this would seem a rather extreme reaction, we will never know the full story of what really drove her to take her own life, but this haunting would seem to be an apparition: a replay of the events that took place on that fateful night.

There have also been inexplicable reports of a Brown Lady that appears to new brides at the hall. She is a friendly lady who appears in the bedroom, smiles at the bride and then disappears. I can only presume she is a long-dead member of one of the numerous generations of illustrious families who still haunts the place and is welcoming the new mistress to the hall.

14

EPWORTH RECTORY

One night it made such a noise in the room over our head as if several people were walking; then... running up and down stairs, and was so outrageous that we thought the children would be frightened, so your father and I rose and went down in the dark to light a candle. Just as we came to the bedroom at the bottom of the broad stairs, having hold of each other, on my side there seemed as if somebody had emptied a bag of money at my feet, and on his as if all the bottles under the stairs had been dashed in a thousand pieces.

John Wesley's mother.

John Wesley, the founder of Methodism, was 13 years old when his elder brother received disturbing news from their family home at Epworth Rectory: the house was haunted by a poltergeist. It is rather strange how although the church does not recognise the existence of ghosts many vicarages and rectories seem to be haunted, including of course Borley Rectory in Essex.

The house was built by Samuel Wesley in 1709 and remained a rectory until 1954. Seven years after he built the property, it was plagued by a poltergeist outbreak, which lasted from December 1716 to January 1717. The main activity was the usual knocking, tapping and groaning, plus the sound of cackling like an old witch, the sound of breaking

Epworth Rectory, home to an active poltergeist in the 18th century.

glass, and also on occasions members of the family felt as if they were being pushed down the stairs. Objects also levitated mysteriously as if moved by unseen hands.

John Wesley's father Samuel used to communicate with the spirit by tapping his stick on the floor, and he would receive a reply in the form of knocks from the ceiling. Most of the Wesley family did not find the poltergeist intimidating, and in fact they affectionately gave it the nickname of 'Old Jeffrey' after an old man who had died there. The only member of the family who was frightened by the ghost was their very large mastiff dog, which Samuel Wesley brought into the house presumably for protection, but of course animals are more sensitive than humans and the poor dog was terrified while in the house. First of all, it barked at the sounds and after a couple of days it would tremble and whine and try to hide behind anyone nearby.

Their manservant Robert Brown was particularly affected by the haunting. He *'heard someone come glaring through the garret to my chamber rattling by my side, as if against my shoes, though I had none there; at other times walking up an down stairs, when all the house were in bed, and gobbling like a turkey cock.'*

The family also caught site of a strange apparition of a man in a loose nightgown trailing behind him. This was often seen by 19-year-old Hetty Wesley, whom the poltergeist seemed to centre on. It is very common in poltergeist cases for them to be attracted to teenage girls. Some say that it is just their emotions due to their age which causes the energy, others that the poltergeist uses the girls' energy to attract attention to itself.

At the end of January 1717 the noises, apparitions and movement stopped. Although a disturbing letter written by Emily Wesley dated 1 April 1717 stated:

'The spirit was with us last night, and heard by many of our family.'

Is it still there to this very day?

15

EAST KIRKBY AIRFIELD

The ghost in man, the ghost that once was man,
But cannot wholly free itself from man,
Are calling to each other thro' a dawn
Stranger than earth has ever seen; the veil
Is rending, and the voices of the day
Are heard across the voices of the dark.
Alfred Lord Tennyson

One of my many theories on ghosts is that for some reason they don't know that they are dead. This applies to many young men killed in battle, especially pilots and aircrew who smashed into the ground at 350 miles an hour, but, before leaving on the mission, believing they had their whole lives still ahead of them. These ghosts are the ones that need help more than any other.

East Kirkby is as haunted as any airfield I know. It was constructed during 1942–43 in the parishes of East Kirkby and Hagnaby, 11 miles north of Boston, and most of the land taken was that of Hagnaby Grange Farm. The farmhouse was left standing within the airfield perimeter track, and due to the building of the airfield a minor road to the east of the site had to be closed. The main contractor was John Laing & Son Ltd.

When ready to receive an operational unit, No. 57 Squadron's Lancasters moved in from Scampton as it was due to be closed for hard runways to be put down in August 1943. The squadron flew its first operation from East Kirkby on the night of 27 August to Hamburg. In November 1943 630 Squadron was formed and remained at East Kirkby until the end of World War Two. At one time over 2,000 servicemen and women were stationed here and huge losses were sustained during the Berlin and Nuremberg raids. In one night, on 11 June 1944, 11 bombers from East Kirkby were lost on a single raid over Germany.

On 17 April, shortly before the end of the war, there was a major accident at East Kirkby when a 1,000lb bomb exploded during bombing up in the darkness, setting off the remainder of the No. 57 Squadron Lancaster's load. This caused a great amount of damage and four people were killed and others injured. Six Lancasters were declared beyond repair and another 14 suffered damage. The nearby hangar and Hagnaby Grange were also badly damaged. In 1945 the last raid from East Kirkby was flown on 25 April. Two hundred and twelve operations were carried out from this airfield, from which, sadly, 121 Lancasters failed to return and another 29 were lost in operational crashes or accidents, and something of these terrifying and tragic events still lingers on here.

In 1981 the airfield was purchased by Fred and Harold Panton and turned into the Lincolnshire Aviation Heritage Centre in memory of their brother, pilot officer Christopher Panton of 433 squadron, who was killed on a raid over Germany in March 1944.

Pride of place in the exhibits is taken by Lancaster NX611, which used to be the gate guard at RAF Scampton. There is also a hangar full of pieces of crashed aircraft dug up from around Lincolnshire, and this wreckage is the actual metal that took many young airman's lives under such traumatic conditions. With such a tragic history it comes as no surprise that the ghostly shadows of lost pilots have been seen here on many occasions, victims of the many air disasters that are just some of the horrors associated with war.

Possibly the most famous ghost of East Kirkby is an airman often seen walking towards the control tower in full flying gear with a trailing parachute. Who is he? Towards the end of the war an American B17 Flying Fortress was in

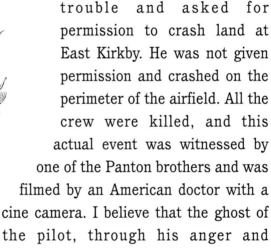

trouble and asked for permission to crash land at East Kirkby. He was not given permission and crashed on the perimeter of the airfield. All the crew were killed, and this actual event was witnessed by one of the Panton brothers and was filmed by an American doctor with a cine camera. I believe that the ghost of the pilot, through his anger and confusion, returns to the control tower to ask why he was not allowed to land and save his crew.

There are also reports of supernatural activity in the control tower itself. Visitors flee the building after sensing a presence, telephones ring even though they are not connected and green lights often appear at night when the building is locked, and none of this activity can ever really be explained.

After spending time at East Kirkby, at about four in the morning I remembered I had left some books in the control tower. I actually looked around to find someone to go back

The control tower at East Kirkby, now the Lincolnshire Aviation Heritage Centre.

in with me; I toyed with the idea of leaving the books rather than go back in on my own. Eventually I threw caution to the wind and entered, ran all the way down the corridor to the room at the bottom, grabbed the books and fled like a scared rabbit.

That's the effect that the haunted control tower of East Kirkby has had on many people.

16

THE ABBEY HOSTEL HOTEL, CROWLAND

Henry Girdlestone was a Fenland farmer; his local pub was the Abbey Hostel Hotel. Henry was a man of his word and one night while sat drinking with his friends he boasted that he could quite easily walk 1,000 miles in as many hours if he ever needed to. 'Go on then,' said one of his drinking partners, 'I will then' said Henry. Everyone in the pub urged him not to be so foolish, but Henry's mind was made up, he was going to do it. Practically everyone in the pub challenged him. Several books were started and the betting was fast and furious. When the last of the wagers had been staked it was agreed that Henry would start walking the following week.

This he did, striding along the flat Lincolnshire roads fairly casually. Sometimes he only walked at a mile an hour, taking a rest whenever he was ahead of his timetable. Slowly the spire of his beloved Crowland Abbey disappeared from his view, as he walked on and on and on. After 200 miles his faithful little terrier dog became lame and could not accompany his master any further, but Henry kept on going, often walking in a trance-like state with his eyes firmly closed but never deviating from the road. After 30 days his health began to cause some concern and those who had challenged him offered to call off their bets. Henry, of course, refused to give up. Forty-nine days after Henry Girdlestone started walking he staggered up to the front door of the

Abbey Hostel Hotel and sank to the floor absolutely exhausted. He had walked 1,025 miles 173 yards and won a sizeable amount of money and the praise of his friends and villagers for miles around.

As the news of Henry's achievements spread, farm hands stopped work in the field and flocked to the pub to toast Henry's success.

Henry died many years after his marathon walk, but it seems that he didn't stop walking and now an apparition has been heard at the Abbey Hostel Hotel, where it all started on 1 February 1844. His ghostly footsteps are often heard clicking along the corridors of the attic. Sometimes his footsteps falter as if he was very weary, but other times they are bold and strong. His ghost has never been seen, but judging by the sounds on the floorboards he is still wearing the same hobnailed boots that he wore in 1844 when he set out on his momentous walk into history.

Crowland Abbey is only about 70 metres from the inn, and Henry is buried in the graveyard. A frightening legend associated with the abbey tells that anyone who walks anticlockwise round the spire of the church will conjure up the devil.

Although slightly less well known, there is also a ghost of a woman in the same hotel as that of Henry who was run over outside the inn and continues to haunt the place. Cold spots have often been experienced in room number five and whenever the door is left open it always closes by itself, slamming shut even though there is nobody there.

17

THE CAMMERINGHAM LIGHT

In the year 61AD, according to Tacitus, 'a severe disaster was sustained in Britain'. The King of the East Anglian Iceni had died.

'His kingdom was plundered by centurions and his private property by slaves, as if they had been captured in war; his widow Boudicca was flogged and his daughters outraged; the chiefs of the Iceni were robbed of their ancestral properties as if the Romans had received the whole country as a gift, and the king's own relatives were reduced to slavery.'

The Iceni, with heroic Boudicca as the leader, revolted and their army headed first for Camulodunum (modern day Colchester), the centre of Roman authority and religion. The town was burned to ashes and everyone Roman or Romano- British was put to the sword. The Romans crack regiment, the Ninth Legion, was stationed at Lincoln and was marching south to the rescue. The victorious Iceni advanced from the sack of Colchester to meet it. By sheer force of numbers, they overcame the Ninth Legion and slaughtered them. Their commander Petilius Cerialis escaped with his horsemen and fled back towards Lincoln, with some of Boudicca's troops in hot pursuit.

The Iceni went on to destroy St Albans and London, killing over 70,000 Romans before being defeated in battle somewhere between London and Chester; the Romans had fought back after gathering together a force of 10,000 men, and when Boudicca was defeated by this impressive tactical army she had no choice but to poison herself. She is believed to be buried somewhere underneath where King's Cross Station now stands and is immortalised in the monument to her memory on the embankment of the Thames, opposite the Houses of Parliament.

Cammeringham is a small village on the b-road between

The monument to Queen Boudicca and her two daughters on the Thames embankment.

Ingham and Lincoln, which runs parallel with the Roman road Ermine Street.

A witness in the early 1900s was walking to work at dawn and saw among the various patches of early morning mist one particularly large block of mist apparently heading towards him. As he stared in horror, he witnessed a chariot drive out of the mist pulled by one white and one black horse. The chariot had what appeared to be swords or blades sticking out from the centre of the wheels. On board was a woman wearing a long flowing dress, bedecked in fine jewellery, whipping the horses furiously. During the whole time that he saw the apparition not a sound was heard.

He is only one of many people in the area that have seen the ghostly chariot believed to be driven by one of the most famous women in British history, Queen Boudicca, known locally as The Cammeringham Light.

Courteous lady, cease to tempt me,
let us end this gentle strife,
I in England have already,
A sweet woman to be my wife.
Then within a nunnery immur'd I'll be.
Daily pray'rs I'll offer for thy love and thee.

If you have ever heard the Dubliners sing this song *The Spanish Lady* you may have wondered about its origins. It is connected to Sir John Bolle of Thorpe Hall in Lincolnshire.

Thorpe Hall is over 400 years old and is situated on the outskirts of Louth. It was built by John Bolle, who in 1566 was occupied with besieging the port of Cadiz with Sir Walter Raleigh and the Earl of Essex. There are some conflicting stories and the events have been tangled as the tales of the tragic events that followed have been passed down the generations. At this time England were at war with Spain, and one of Elizabeth's soldiers fighting the Spanish was Sir John Bolle. He was captured and imprisoned in Spain. While in prison, he was regularly visited by a Spanish noblewoman, Donna Leonora Oviedo, who brought him food, extra clothing and blankets, although some stories and indeed the song suggest that she was taken captive by Sir John. After a while they fell in love and she would have done anything for her

Thorpe Hall is haunted by the ghostly figure of a woman who stabbed herself in the heart.

lover. He persuaded her to use some of her jewellery to bribe the gaolers to turn a blind eye to his release, which she did, risking her own life to secure his freedom. She then used the last of her jewels to buy a passage for him back to England. She had expected to go to England with Sir John, but he told her that he was already married and she would have to stay behind, but he would send for her later. He never did send for her, and in desperation she climbed on board a ship for England, turning up at Thorpe Hall dressed in a beautiful green ball gown, only to find Sir John happily reunited with his wife. In total despair and disbelief, she committed suicide by stabbing herself through the heart underneath the oak tree in the grounds of the hall, heartbroken by Sir John's actions.

There is another line of thought that suggests that Sir John met Donna Leonora while in Cadiz, where he was given a knighthood for his bravery, and he won her heart, but because he was happily married he refused to compromise himself with her. When Sir John left to return to England she insisted that he take a portrait of her with him, in which she was dressed in a green dress, and some gifts for his wife as a mark of her respect for her. Sir John then started to lay a place for Donna Leonora at his table at Thorpe Hall in her honour, while she spent the rest of her days in a convent, where she died 10 years later.

Her ghost has often been seen, always in a green dress, around the old oak tree, wandering around looking for John in the hope that one day they can be together again. She has also been seen on the road outside this 400-year-old hall. Drivers have been known to stop to offer her a lift, but she never gets in. One day a man on a bike had to swerve to miss her. He fell off and jumped up in a rage to give her a telling off only to find himself quite alone in the road.

As time passes by there have been fewer sightings of the Spanish Lady. Perhaps if she is only a recording that plays over and over again, just like your favourite video if played enough it will eventually fade into oblivion.

19

MARTON CHURCH, GAINSBOROUGH

Marton is a tiny hamlet situated at a fork with the old Roman road, the A1500 and the A156. In 1891 its church was restored and rebuilt. It is quite common for builders to see and hear ghosts during demolition and rebuilding, and I have heard many stories from builders in my time as a paranormal historian. Through my experiences and these accounts, I am lead to believe that what they are seeing or hearing is a recording from the past stored in the fabric of the building. All buildings made of stone or bricks contain silica water and iron oxide, all properties used in recording studios. When buildings undergo structural changes, it is like knocking a cassette recorder on the floor; sometimes the jolt causes it to come on.

When the church was rebuilt there were many reports from the builders of a woman in grey drifting through the door and vanishing, and these accounts concern a presence rather than a recording.

When a new vicar took over he started to sense an elderly man with a bald patch but with white flowing hair over his ears at every communion. He was always wearing a dark green cassock. The vicar confided in some of the parishioners, stating that he wasn't sure whether he was seeing the figure or if it was all in his mind.

One day when he was talking to a very elderly member of

the congregation about his experiences, she looked quite shocked as she explained to him that after the church was rebuilt in 1891 it adopted a colour scheme of green and red and the choir were given dark green cassocks and she actually remembered a member of the choir from the turn of the century who fitted the description perfectly.

20

THE GARDEN HOUSE HOTEL, ST MARTIN'S, STAMFORD

A shadow flits before me
Not thou, but like to thee:
Ah Christ, that it was possible
For one short hour to see
The souls we loved, that they might tell us
What and where they be.
Alfred Lord Tennyson

Close to the centre of Stamford, the Garden House hotel, situated next to Burghley Park, was built in 1796 possibly as a coaching inn. Overlooking an acre of walled, formal gardens, it now boasts 21 well furnished en-suite bedrooms, but some of them are believed to be haunted, especially the top floor, as this is believed to have been the servants quarters in days long ago and is now guest rooms 18, 19, 20 and 21. Housekeeping staff regularly sense a feeling of sadness in all of the four rooms, and things move of their own accord and curtains draw to and fro on their own. Dark shadows also appear, and a figure has been seen looking in through the window of room 18, which of course would be impossible for an ordinary person to do as the room is on the second floor. Room 18 is also reputed to be haunted by a man who has breathing problems, as heavy laboured breathing has been heard by guests staying in the room without any other explanation for the noises.

If you are looking for a haunted hotel in Lincolnshire you need look no further than the Garden House Hotel. One day we may even find out who the ghosts are and why they still dwell there, but no records have been found so far.

The Garden House Hotel where strange shadows and other paranormal activity have been experienced in the attic bedrooms.

21

THE LINCOLNSHIRE WETLANDS

Axholme is a river island bounded on the eastern side by the Trent, and on the northern and north western sides by the old River Don, which flowed by Crowle, Luddington and Garthorpe into the Trent and formed in part of its course the boundary between Lincolnshire and Yorkshire. The old rivers Torne and Idle formed the western boundary.

The name Axholme is a corruption of Axel-holme formed from the name of the principal place Axel (now Haxey, a mere village), and holme, which was used by the Saxons to denote a river-island.

In the middle ages Axholme was covered with marshes, especially in the western and southern parts. The isle was drained in the 17th century, but before that there were pools of black water and wetlands. Many people died here on dark nights when the paths were not visible, and this encouraged the development of stories and legends that there are evil spirits in the area luring people to their fates as they travel along the deadly paths.

Stories abound of death and evil in all of the Lincolnshire wetlands before they were drained. Many were afraid to cross them, and even more so when a local lad, Tom Pattison, who was not superstitious, walked around the wetlands to prove there was nothing out there. Some of the young lads in the area started to believe that Tom was right and there was nothing out there, and on that night they decided they would follow him. As Tom continued a cold, damp chill came over from the sea and the wind started to howl around him. Suddenly his lantern was blown out and the hidden explorers began to feel real fear. The evil of the wetlands began to surround Tom and the lads behind could see shadows moving and hear wailing and screaming noises. They lost sight of Tom but could still hear his cries. A light appeared, and they caught sight of Tom hanging on to a tree branch, his face deathly white. His other hand was in the grip of a bodyless hand as he tried to hold on to the branch. This was known as the death hand, and with an horrendous cry Tom disappeared into the water. The boys ran home terrified by what they had seen. The months passed by then one day Tom reappeared in the exact same spot that his body had been dragged under the water, but his arm was missing and he would not speak so no one knows what happened to him in the months he was missing. He was so affected by his experience that he died within a year in his mother's lap, and she too died at the same time. They say that Tom still haunts the old marshland on dark cold nights even though they are now drained, and his mother is often seen trailing behind him.

2 2

GUNBY HALL,
BURGH LE MARSH

And one, an English home-gray twilight pour'd
On dewy pastures, dewy trees,
Softer than sleep-all things in order stored,
A haunt of ancient Peace.
from *The Palace of Art*, Alfred Lord Tennyson

This magnificent house was built in 1700 for Sir William Massingberd and is located on the edge of the Lincolnshire Wolds. It has been lived in by many generations of families over the years and is reported to have spirit residents as well. Housed between the walls, among the wood panelled rooms, oak staircase and fine paintings and furniture are ghosts, and almost in way of proof is an original verse written by the hand of Alfred Lord Tennyson, still preserved in the house to this day. This verse is a very apt description of the house as it ends with these words: 'A haunt of ancient peace'.

But peace has not always reigned in this ancient house according to the story of forbidden love centred around here, which resulted in a bloody and callous murder taking place not long after it was built. It appears that either the wife of Sir William or, more likely, his daughter fell in love with one of his Lordship's footmen. Marriage could never be permitted between the daughter of a peer of the realm and a servant, and in desperation they planned to elope. His Lordship, unfortunately for the couple, found out and caught them just as they were about to leave. In his rage, he murdered the young footman and dumped his body in the pond near to the house. The unhappy soul of the murdered man still haunts the pathway alongside the pond, and to this very day it is still known as 'The Ghost Walk'.

There is also talk of another haunting on the same path, that of a man and woman walking arm in arm. There is always a drop in temperature and a sense of sadness felt just before they appear, after a few

Alfred Lord Tennyson, whose haunting poem aptly describes Gunby Hall.

moments the shades disappear, the temperature and atmosphere then return to normal. Is it the ghosts of the two lovers united in death but never in life?

FURTHER RESEARCH

If you have been caught by the ghost-hunting bug after reading about our adventures in Lincolnshire, the following publications and DVDs may be of interest to you.

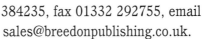

Books:

The Ghost Tour of Great Britain: Derbyshire with Richard Felix, Breedon Books, 2005.

The Ghost Tour of Great Britain: Wales with Richard Felix, Breedon Books, 2005.

The Ghost Tour of Yorkshire: with Richard Felix, Breedon Books, 2005.

The above books are available from all good bookshops and may also be purchased direct from the publishers, Breedon Books, 3 The Parker Centre, Mansfield Road, Derby, DE21 4SZ, tel 01332 384235, fax 01332 292755, email sales@breedonpublishing.co.uk.

DVDs

This DVDs, as well as many others from the Ghost Tour of Great Britain, are available from shops in Derby and direct from the producers, Films Factory, 61 Mill Lane, Belper, DE56 1LH, tel 01773 880620. Order online at: www.filmsfactory.co.uk

INDEX